"Having guided dozens of Doctor of Ministry students through research projects for over ten years, I can attest to the fact that achieving quality design of assessment tools—and accomplishing proper interpretation of survey results—can present considerable challenges to students. Geoff Sutton's *Creating Surveys*, with each chapter's clear objectives, well-organized content, and chapter summaries, will serve research students, professionals, and community leaders well in their efforts to better understand the necessary components and methodologies for gaining desired information and presenting it in a way that reflects critical thinking about survey results."

—Dr. Lois E. Olena, Associate Professor and Doctor of Ministry Project Coordinator, Assemblies of God Theological Seminary

"In this day and age, being on the cutting edge is more important than ever. Science allows us to better understand the world around us and effectively impact change, innovation, and growth. Yet, many are intimidated by the confusing process of gathering and interpreting empirical data and give up before they even begin. Creating Surveys simplifies this process and can help researchers, professionals, students, and lay people alike easily access data that can be used to affect change in the future. I only wish that this resource was around when I was a graduate student!"

—Luke J. Davidiuk, PsyD, Capt., USAF, BSC
ADAPT Element Chief, Vandenberg AFB, CA

CREATING SURVEYS
Evaluating Programs and Reading Research

Geoffrey W. Sutton

CREATING SURVEYS
Evaluating Programs and
Reading Research

Geoffrey W. Sutton
Sunflower Press
ISBN: 9781522012726

To those who have encouraged me in conducting research—

Thurman Vanzant, Evangel University
James R. Koller, University of Missouri-Columbia
Everett L. Worthington, Jr., Virginia Commonwealth University
E. Grant Jones, Evangel University

Table of Contents

Introduction

People have been conducting surveys since the first person asked a question. We want to know what others think and feel. We want to know the best places to visit and where to get a good deal. Whether your school, organization, or place of worship has ten or ten thousand people, their ideas, beliefs, attitudes, practices, opinions, and commitments can help leaders make informed decisions. Surveys also help us understand what people have learned following a workshop, seminar, or other educational program. Of course, surveys are also part of formal research projects.

Surveys are ways to collect information. The information obtained from surveys can be used to describe, compare, contrast, predict, or explain something about how people think, feel, and act.

This book is about creating surveys and reading survey research. It is aimed at leaders and students in many fields who have not had extensive coursework and experience in research methods and statistics.

What is the purpose of this book?

You have probably seen a lot of surveys and found some are written or organized better than others. My primary purpose in this book is to help people create better surveys. I also hope to help readers evaluate news stories and reports of surveys. Even if you never create a survey, I hope you learn more about the usefulness and limitations of surveys.

The readers most likely to find this book helpful are leaders in schools, universities, or organizations that serve people in such places as small businesses, community centers, and churches. Another category of readers who can benefit from this book is students—in a variety of fields—who will conduct a survey as a part of a research project in undergraduate or graduate programs. Readers need not have prior knowledge of statistics or research methods to benefit from this book. I hope this book will be of value to the following people.

Administrators

Leaders in any organization often read and participate in surveys. This book can help you better understand survey research whether you are reading the work of others or creating your own projects. In addition, many school administrators, agency CEOs, and clergy receive requests to conduct research on their campuses. This book will help you evaluate such requests.

Health Care Professionals

Counselors, social workers, psychologists, chaplains, and other licensed professionals are often conducting survey research or serving as team members on research projects. This book will help you review basic concepts typically taught in research methods textbooks. If you are consulting on a project, you may find this book useful to recommend to team members who are new to survey methods.

Educational Professionals

If you have not had coursework on survey research, this book can help you create projects to engage students, supplement your own research, or contribute to other projects in your school or professional organization.

Students

Undergraduate and graduate students can benefit from a review of the basic concepts covered in this book. This book does not cover the details you would find in a graduate research methods textbook, but it does review many of the key concepts needed to read and understand research and create survey projects. I hope this book is especially useful to students in disciplines that do not typically include an intensive sequence of research and statistics courses.

Community Leaders

Chances are you have seen a survey report in a news source or heard someone quote the results of a survey. This book can help you learn more about the survey process, participate as a team member on a research project, and think more critically about published research.

How can I use this book?

This book is designed to help people create surveys and think critically about survey results. Surveys can provide useful information, but the results can also be misinterpreted. Following are some ways to use this book.

Create surveys to evaluate a workshop or other program

Many organizations offer beneficial programs and services to the public, but many lack data demonstrating the effectiveness of their services. Leaders need to decide whether to renew or change existing programs or create new ones. People vote with their feet. Programs and services that are not helpful die for lack of support. Surveys can provide vital information about the needs of a student body, a community, or the membership in a church before creating a program that ignores critical needs. Surveys can help assess the importance of a program from the perspective of those it is designed to serve. This book offers guidance on different ways to evaluate a workshop or other educational presentations and community services.

Create surveys to assess changes in attitudes, beliefs, or knowledge

I have attended many educational programs. Some are better than others. Following a program, I have often been asked to give my opinion about the speaker, objectives, and setting. Sometimes I have been asked what I have learned. Educational programs help people learn more about their profession as well as life-changing events. People may learn to cope with loss, forgive others, prepare for marriage, improve their marriage, or become better parents. Programs can help lay people become better teachers, leaders, and crisis workers. Programs may also address other important issues, like sexual harassment, money management, and church security. This book includes examples of survey items that address opinions, attitudes, beliefs, and knowledge.

Create surveys to help with decisions about a building project

Organizations often need to make decisions about new buildings, remodeling, and relocating. Well-designed surveys can be quick and effective methods to obtain useful information. In addition to gauging attitudinal and financial support, survey items can help leaders decide on important features to include in a new project. Often, people who are not directly involved in building plans have specific knowledge that can be of great benefit before planning has gone too far. At later stages, people may be asked to vote on color schemes or other details involving options. This book can help you select ways to word your survey questions.

Create surveys to understand people
As organizations grow it can be useful to better understand members by collecting some basic information. Collecting information need not be intrusive. Just knowing some facts like age, sex, education, ethnicity, and occupation can provide some basic ways to think about "who we are as an organization." In a short survey, it is easy to add a few questions to better understand the members' opinions regarding important aspects of the organization. By the end of this book, you will find many examples of questions you may want to ask.

Learn ways to evaluate survey research
Survey reports are everywhere. The findings from surveys are commonly reported in news media, magazines, and books. This book can help you think more critically about research reports. You will learn how surveys may be helpful. And you will learn how survey results can be misinterpreted. You will gain a basic conceptual understanding of the statistics found in journal articles.

What are some reasons *not* to buy this book?

It may sound strange to talk about reasons not to buy this book, but the fact is, this book is not for everyone. I refer to various statistical procedures, but I do not explain how to do the calculations. Instead, I provide a reader's conceptual approach to statistics. Similarly, if you need a detailed text covering a variety of research designs, this book will not meet that need. I refer to basic experimental studies with two or three groups and only briefly comment on advanced research methods like Structural Equation Modeling. This book can be used in undergraduate and graduate courses where students either do not need to know how to design and analyze complex research studies or get those advanced skills in other courses.

How are surveys administered?

Surveys can be administered in several ways. After an online survey has been created, links can be posted on online pages or in online groups. Survey links can be sent in emails or messages. Some companies offer easy-to-create surveys within their online pages. Alternatively, people can complete surveys on any available screen in a classroom, hallway, or public place.

Surveys may be presented in a more personal way. For example, an interviewer can meet with people online, by phone, or in person. The interview can be conducted with one person or a group.

Older methods of conducting surveys include sending paper questionnaires through the mail or asking people to complete paper forms in a public place. These older methods continue to exist because they reach people who may be missed by other methods.

What is a survey?

In this book, I primarily use the word *survey* to mean an organized set of items designed to collect information from *respondents*—people who respond to the items. A *survey item* is usually either a statement or a question. People use many different terms for groups of items that can be called a survey. Here are a few examples: polls, questionnaires, quizzes, tests, inventories, scales, and measures. A *poll* is often associated with elections but can simply mean a set of questions used to gather an opinion. *Questionnaire* and *inventory* are other words for sets of items used to collect responses. *Measure* is a generic term used by researchers who report the way they assessed characteristics of people in a research study. The measures may include collections of items called surveys, inventories, scales, and tests.

The term *quiz* is usually reserved for a brief, informal, assessment of knowledge. A test is like a quiz but is usually longer. Tests cover a wide range of human characteristics, including knowledge, intelligence, memory, personality, and athletic skills. Many tests are published after research methods have established that their scores are reliable and valid for the purposes claimed by the test publisher.

How is this book organized?

I organized the chapters in this book into three sections. In *Part I: Planning a Survey*, I present information to guide you through the process of creating a survey and getting it ready to collect information. You will learn to create a purpose statement, strategies for reviewing previous research, how to write items, tips on organization and formatting, and elements of common approval processes, which include considering survey ethics. The last chapter in part one suggests ways to get respondents.

In *Part II: Using Surveys to Understand People*, I present a six-dimensional model that addresses most aspects of human nature. I refer to the six dimensions using the acronym SCOPES: Social Context (e.g., age, sex, gender, ethnicity, other cultural factors), Cognition (thinking, beliefs, opinions), Observable behavior patterns or traits, Physical health, Emotions and feelings, and Spirituality or religiosity. This multidimensional model is sensitive to people from diverse cultural backgrounds. Each chapter includes examples of survey items that measure different aspects of the six dimensions.

The final section, *Part III: Understanding Basic Designs and Statistics*, begins with an example of how to evaluate a workshop or similar educational program. Then I present a summary of basic statistics with an emphasis on reading research results rather than calculating them. Two chapters deal with topics of reliability and validity. And the final chapter offers some tips on presenting your survey results.

Key Features of *Creating Surveys*

- Learning objectives for each chapter
- Concise chapter summaries
- Short chapters covering essential survey topics
- Many items to use in building your own projects
- Examples of text to introduce and close surveys
- How-to guide for evaluating workshops and seminars
- New concept list following chapter summaries
- Numerous references to online resources
- Reader's guide to statistics and data analyses
- Information on ethics and project approval
- Examples of tables and charts for reports
- Extensive research glossary
- Extended Table of Contents
- Link to book website resources

Style Note

This book is written in a modified APA style designed to be reader-friendly. For the benefit of those familiar with APA style, I will note some differences. I use italics rather than quotation marks for emphasis as well as for terms and statistics. I limit the use of quotation marks to only indicate direct quotes. Rather than interrupt the text with long reference citations, I have mostly limited the in-text citations to one or two authors with dates, except when more authors are needed to identify the full reference, which you will find in the reference section at the back of this book. Similarly, I have placed most lengthy internet links in notes at the end of a chapter on in an appendix rather than interrupt the text. The tables and figures are designed for this publication format and do not follow the APA manuscript guidelines.

Summary

The primary purpose of this book is to help readers create better surveys. A secondary purpose is to help readers learn how to evaluate survey reports and contribute as knowledgeable team members on survey projects.

Creating Surveys offers a readers' guide to basic research methods and statistics.

Survey is a broad term that includes polls, questionnaires, quizzes, tests, inventories, scales, and measures.

Part I:
Planning A Survey

1. Focusing on a Purpose

Objectives:

> Explain how a question can help clarify the purpose of a survey.
>
> Identify the relationship of goals to secondary questions.

Have you ever been to a couples' retreat or marriage seminar? Over the years I have provided couples counseling and kept up with research on what seems to help couples enjoy each other in their relationship. So, it was a pleasant surprise when I was asked to conduct an evaluation of a workshop program focused on Christian marriages. The leaders often received positive feedback about the program. What was needed was some quantifiable data to examine along with the qualitative remarks. Consultation on such projects is a collaborative effort. I provided sample questions related to their goal of understanding what participants found helpful and their overall level of satisfaction. We also wanted to know a little bit about the participants. Following the completion of the final draft, the leaders administered the questionnaires. I entered the data into a spreadsheet and calculated some statistics, which I included in a report.

The story illustrates some points about planning. We need to know what we are going to evaluate. Existing programs usually have a statement of purpose and goals that can guide us. Sometimes it is helpful to work with a consultant for one or more aspects of a survey project.

Before creating a survey, decide on what you hope to accomplish. Researchers often begin by identifying a need, like evaluating a couples' enrichment workshop, assessing support

for a sex education program, obtaining feedback on a new organizational policy, or identifying community needs. Most researchers think it best to turn survey topics into statements of
purpose before creating a survey. The next step is to reframe
the purpose statement as a primary question. Questions help us
focus on finding answers. Primary questions are broad enough
that people will think of many answers. Following are examples of purposes and primary questions.

> Purpose: To evaluate a marriage enrichment program.
> Question: How effective is the marriage enrichment pro-
> gram?

> Purpose: To develop a multipurpose family event center.
> Question: What needs should a multipurpose family event
> center meet?

When you consider broad purposes like improving community relations or expanding educational programs, it is possible to think about many secondary questions that need to be
answered. At first, it is good to generate a long list of secondary questions to ask. Eventually, a research team can edit the
list to focus on those secondary questions related to the primary question.

In program evaluation research, secondary questions are
usually related to program goals. Thus, it will be important to
establish the purpose and goals of a program before creating a
survey. More complex programs include objectives associated
with each goal. In these cases, you can see that every objective
can be turned into a question providing a detailed evaluation
of a workshop, educational course, or other program.

What is Your Purpose?

In this section, I provide examples of different questions that can be asked to gain different kinds of information about a topic. The following paragraphs will illustrate how the same topic can be addressed in different ways.

Forgiveness Education Example

I have studied and presented programs on forgiveness in churches and at conferences. Forgiveness is a broad topic that can be approached from religious and secular perspectives. Forgiveness is a virtue of faith and important to personal well-being and healthy relationships. People often confuse forgiveness with reconciliation. There are many questionnaires about forgiveness that I can use in a survey, but the questionnaires all have different questions or items reflecting different definitions of forgiveness. A religious forgiveness program may include scriptures dealing with forgiveness, personal stories of forgiveness, and suggestions about how to forgive others. Following a workshop, respondents may have learned academic content, personal strategies to be more forgiving, strategies to help others forgive, or even a personal application—letting go of old hurts. The purpose of any survey should consider the purpose of the forgiveness program and clearly define any terms. Our primary purpose may be to simply evaluate a forgiveness workshop, but the following secondary questions illustrate additional questions of interest.

Following are some examples of questions that could lead to creating different types of forgiveness surveys:

- How did participants like the forgiveness seminar?

- What did participants learn at the forgiveness workshop?
- What do the participants believe about forgiveness?
- Do participants view forgiveness as different from reconciliation?
- How well are participants prepared to help others learn the steps to forgiveness?

You may notice that even the secondary questions in the list of forgiveness questions can generate another level of questions. For example, consider the many questions you could ask to answer the question: What did participants learn at the forgiveness workshop? To answer that question, we would need to examine facts and principles about forgiveness. But we could also ask about beliefs and attitudes if those were included in the workshop.

Marriage Programs Example

Many churches and organizations offer programs to help couples with some aspect of their marriage. Marriage is a broad topic. Following a weekend program, respondents may be asked to complete a questionnaire to evaluate the workshop, but what should be asked? We could ask questions to see how much they remembered or what changes they intend to make in their relationship. We could ask how well they liked the program, the speakers, the refreshments, the facility, or just get an overall impression of satisfaction. The primary purpose of a marriage survey will be tied to the primary purpose of the program or research project. A survey may have a few related purposes, such as evaluating learning and satisfaction. Different surveys may be more focused on understanding marriage.

Again, the best programs and projects have statements of purpose and goals. Secondary questions usually relate to program or project goals.

Following are some examples of questions that could lead to creating different types of marriage surveys:

- How effective was the premarital counseling seminar?
- What factors reduce the likelihood of divorce?
- How satisfied were the participants with the couples' workshop?
- What books have couples found most helpful in their marriage?
- Was the setting suitable for the marriage enrichment event?
- What are the most important things seminar participants learned about marriage?
- How do principles of faith support marriage?
- How well did the participants learn to manage conflict?

Policy and Procedures Example

Organizations need policies to address security and safety. Some policies are better than others. A survey could focus on elements to include in a policy and its procedures or evaluate how well people can understand or remember an existing policy and procedures. The purpose of the survey will depend on what we want to do with the information. For example, do we want to create or modify a policy, or do we wish to assess the need for an educational program to help members who may or may not know what they need to know to keep themselves and others safe?

Following are some examples of questions that could lead to creating different types of surveys about policies and procedures:

- What do people know about our safety policy?
- How well do our staff and membership know our policy and procedures about sexual harassment?
- How well do students know our procedures for responding to an active shooter on campus?
- How well do people know our procedures for dealing with a concern?
- How well do faculty, staff, and students know our policy on behavior?
- How much do stakeholders know about our scholarship program?
- How well do employees understand our benefits policy?

Summary
Some surveys are short and to the point while others are far-reaching. And some are just confusing. It's best to create focused surveys. Focused surveys ask questions designed to accomplish one primary goal.

Effective surveys are focused on one topic framed as a statement of purpose and an associated primary question. Secondary questions relate to project goals. A few questions may be needed to address each goal.

When using surveys to evaluate complex projects, look for objectives linked to the goals, which may be reworded as survey questions.

2. Learning from Previous Research

Objectives:
>Identify major sources of survey results.
>Identify databases containing survey research articles.
>Describe the sections of research articles.
>Briefly describe different types of data analysis strategies.

Before writing items to include in your survey, it is a good idea to look at what has already been done. In this chapter, I will suggest ways you can discover previously published studies. Next, I will review the common components of research reports. Finally, I will provide a brief conceptual overview of some complex data analyses found in academic journals.

Finding Previous Research

The Gallup company is well known for their surveys, which often appear in news stories throughout the year. Early in 2017 they released the results of a survey titled, "Views of Origin of Human Beings," which they have repeated for years. By using the same questions, they are able to show changes in beliefs over time. Their work is easy to locate online. And it is easy to read because they provide simple tables and charts with statistics most people understand. For example, they offered several opinions about the role of God in creation or evolution. Positive responses to the item, "Humans evolved, but God had no part," were 19% in 2017 but only 9% in 1982.

You can find a lot of survey questions using search engines if you know what you are looking for. Begin with a survey topic and words or short phrases related to your topic. Several companies report the results of surveys dealing with a variety of topics, such as politics, well-being, and religion. Following are some organizations that report the results of surveys. Their project summaries can help you think about current topics and how they can be addressed using surveys.

- Gallup: www.gallup.com
- Pew Research Center: www.pewforum.org
- Hartford Institute for Religion Research: hirr.hartsem.edu
- Public Religion Research Institute: www.prri.org

Several research databases have collections of research articles and books relevant to the focus of this book. They include Proquest, ERIC, PsycINFO, SocINDEX, EBSCO, PsycARTICLES, PsycBOOKS, and PyscTESTS. These and other databases are usually available from university libraries. If the above-mentioned resources are new to you, plan to consult a librarian for guidance in searching publications relevant to your project.

I did not mention news sources or magazines because the variety of research published can be limited to what their readership is likely to read. Also, although such sources often publish summaries of research, they do not usually publish the details that appear in journal articles. Research summaries in newspapers and magazines can be helpful, but they are no substitute for reading the original research, which has been subject to review by other researchers. You will also need to search academic journals to find rare or conflicting research that may not have appeared in popular news outlets. Because articles in academic journals can be difficult to read, I will comment on the parts of a research article in the next section.

Identifying the Sections in Research Articles

In this part of the chapter, I present a brief description of the content often found in the sections of a research article: abstract, introduction with literature review, method, results, discussion, and references.

Abstract

Research articles being with a paragraph summarizing the entire article. The abstract describes the study, provides select information about the sample, and includes a summary of the results. You can use the abstract as a way of deciding if the article is relevant to your study.

Introduction

The first one or two paragraphs in an article introduce readers to the study. Often, you will not see the word *introduction*. The introduction provides an overview of the primary research question or questions and states why the study is important.

Literature Review

The literature review follows the introductory paragraph or paragraphs. Like the introduction, there is no heading called *literature review*. Authors organize literature reviews in different ways. Often, they will summarize older research in one paragraph before focusing attention on research that deals with the variables in the present study.

Variables are characteristics that can vary in more than one way, like attitudes, opinions, personality traits, and beliefs.

In experiments, *independent variables* are controlled by the researchers. Examples of independent variables include different kinds of workshops, methods of teaching, leadership styles, or counseling interventions. *Dependent variables* are characteristics that change as a result of an independent variable. Dependent variables are often measured using surveys. For example, we may be interested in surveys demonstrating the effectiveness of a premarital workshop or the value of a group to help people cope with loss.

Near the end of the literature review, the authors will provide a summary that shows how previous research relates to the primary purpose of their study. They will then list their *hypotheses*, which are statements about what they hope to find. Hypotheses are analogous to goal statements and secondary questions related to an overall project purpose.

Method

The method section contains the details of the study. The method section should include enough detail to help you carry out the same study with your own sample. You should find a description of the people in the study, called *participants*. Some studies provide more details than others. You will usually find information about age, sex, geographic location, ethnicity, and other pertinent characteristics.

Next are subsections on materials and, if relevant, any apparatus that was used. Materials can include workshop manuals and videos. Apparatuses can include specific equipment that was used and how it was used. For example, researchers can present surveys using tablets, cell phones, or paper forms. Surveys may be administered during face-to-face interviews, online, or in a focus group.

Another important part of the method section is a subsection on measures. In survey research, measures are tests or questionnaires. A large survey may have subgroups of three to five items that measure—ask questions about—a specific subtopic linked to the overall purpose. Researchers report the name of the test or questionnaire along with a sample question and information about reliability and validity.

When you find a study similar to what you are planning, the method section can provide helpful ideas about what you could do in your own study.

Results

The results section is one that is often skipped by those who have not studied the advanced statistical procedures common in contemporary research articles. For this reason, I've provided a section on reading research results to help you gain some familiarity with the different types of data analyses you may find in complex articles.

Discussion

Following the results section, the authors summarize the results and show how their findings relate to the work of other researchers. The discussion section is the place to explain the results in terms of theory and/or previous studies. Some results may support the researchers' hypotheses and be consistent with others' research. Some results may be different from what the researchers expected or different from what others have found. It is the responsibility of the authors to explain why the differences may have occurred. Finally, the discussion section is the place where the authors suggest ideas for future research and report the limitations of their study. Their ideas for future research can help you create your own project. The limitations subsection may help you avoid problems the authors encountered.

References

The reference section can provide you with other studies or articles relevant to your survey project. If you begin with a recent article, the reference list should include many of the articles that were available at the time the authors wrote their article. This can save you considerable time in searching databases. In addition, reference lists can provide you with the names of authors and journals that will help you narrow your search for additional articles. You may also find articles containing questions you can use in your survey.

Reading Basic Research Results

In this part of the chapter, I expand on the results section of an article by describing some data analysis techniques common in contemporary research studies. I will provide more details about basic statistics in later chapters. My focus here is to help you get some sense of the complex array of data analyses that can be puzzling to many students and professionals who do not specialize in data analysis.

Descriptive Statistics

Authors usually begin the results section with descriptive statistics that summarize basic survey results. You may find percentages of people who answered survey questions in different ways based on grouping variables like age and sex. For example, in a report of a survey of people attending colleges, you may learn what percentage of home-schooled women and men attend Christian versus secular colleges.

Descriptive statistics also include measures of central tendency such as the mode, median, and mean. These are described in more detail in later chapters. The *mode* is the most frequent score, the *median* is the middle score, and the *mean* is the arithmetic average of a set of scores.

Correlations

Correlations are values that describe the strength and direction of a relationship. A common correlation is the *Pearson r,* sometimes just reported as an *r* value. The *r* values range from -1.00 through zero to +1.00. Positive numbers are reported without the plus sign and represent a positive relationship between two variables. For example, people high in gratitude are also high in forgiveness (Dwiwardani et al., 2014). Negative values represent opposite trends such that as one score increases, the other score decreases. In my experience, increased absences from a statistics class are negatively correlated with scores on statistics tests. As one variable increases (absences), the other variable decreases (scores on statistics tests).

Tests of Hypotheses and Effects

Researchers use a variety of tests to address the hypotheses reported in their articles. The results of statistical tests are worded such that they either *support* or *fail to support* the research hypotheses. The logic of hypothesis testing can be confusing. After researchers formulate their hypotheses, which are statement about what they think is true, they concurrently form a null hypothesis that assumes no difference.

Here's an example: Suppose we thought a sign would make a difference in how much people respect signs about taking things from parks. We could try out two different messages. We may have hypothesized that a new message is more effective than the one that isn't working. In a classic study, Robert Cialdini (2003) observed that the existing sign about not picking up the tons of petrified wood in Arizona's Petrified Forest National Park wasn't working. He and his colleagues tried other signs and found that simply asking visitors not to take the wood was more effective. A null hypothesis assumes no difference between the signs or any other comparison we wish to examine. If the results show there is a difference, we reject the null hypothesis and find support for the research hypothesis. If the results are about the same, we fail to reject the null hypothesis and simultaneously fail to find support for our idea—the research hypothesis. Note that scientists do not prove their hypotheses; when things go as planned, they find support. By the way, in the park study, people who saw the sign about the loss of tons of petrified wood taken each year took far more marked wood out of the park than those in the "do not take" group.

All statistics have some degree of error. Traditionally, researchers want to be at least 95% confident that their findings are reliable. When researchers report findings as significant, they often mean there is less than a small percentage of the time that similar results would not be obtained. The wording includes a probability value referred to as p. A statement that a finding is less than .05 ($p < .05$) means a statistical value as large or larger would only likely be found 5% of the time. Some researchers wish to use a higher level of confidence, so you may see $p < .01$, representing a less than 1% likelihood of a chance finding. You can think of statistical significance as a statement about the reliability of a finding.

Statistical tests are reported along with effect sizes (*ES*). An effect size indicates the strength of the relationship between the independent variable and the dependent variable. Effect sizes are more important than the results of hypothesis testing.

As a matter of clarity, researchers find *support* for hypotheses rather than *proof*. Survey research does not result in certainty—only varying degrees of confidence. Similarly, negative findings are usually worded to indicate failure to support a hypothesis. Unless a study was designed to test competing hypotheses, it is not reasonable to say that the lack of support for the stated hypothesis automatically means another hypothesis was supported.

t test

There are a few types of *t* tests, which I will cover in chapter 16. Essentially, the *t* test produces a *t* value that helps researchers decide if there is a statistically significant difference between two sets of scores. The researchers may be comparing survey scores from two different groups or survey scores from the same group taken at two different times, such as before and after a workshop. A *t* test can also be used to compare current results to previously established values, such as the average score for your organization over the past decade.

The *t* test and other statistical tests are reported along with effect sizes (*ES*). Again, an effect size indicates the strength of the relationship between the independent variable and the dependent variable. A common effect size associated with *t* tests is Cohen's *d*.

ANOVA

There are several types of ANOVA procedures. The term *ANOVA* refers to *Analysis of Variance*. *Variance* is a statistical term we will review later. Variance refers to differences, so the

ANOVA procedures examine differences in scores among groups of people who complete a survey. For example, an ANOVA can be used to assess different levels of membership satisfaction by people who experience three or four different leadership styles. The ANOVA procedure is usually reported with an F value. The larger the F value, the more likely it is that the differences the researchers found are not due to chance.

There may be several independent variables in a project. The effect of each variable is tested with an F test. When there are two or more variables, researchers also test for possible interaction effects, which results in additional F tests for each interaction. *Interactions* refer to the possibility that two or more variables combine to produce a change in the dependent variable. As with t tests, researchers include a probability (p) value with each F test. A common effect size associated with F tests is partial eta squared. ANOVA is used when there are one or more independent variables but only one dependent variable.

ANCOVA
ANCOVA is a procedure like ANOVA except researchers can study the effects of one or more independent variables on a dependent variable after adjusting for other variables, called *covariates*, which were not a primary focus of the study. The letter C in ANCOVA stands for *covariate*. There can be several covariates in a study. In testing for differences among groups experiencing different leadership styles, we could study the effects on satisfaction after adjusting for a covariate of years of employment. A key word in ANCOVA studies is *adjusting*. Analysts adjust the scores based on information about the covariate before testing for significant differences.

Regression

Regression is a statistical procedure used to predict values on a *criterion* variable from the knowledge of values obtained on a *predictor* variable. For example, an organization may use an employment screening test or survey that has been useful in the past to predict how well employees perform a particular type of job. The criterion variable is a *continuous variable,* meaning it can have a range of score values. Predictor variables may be either continuous or categorical variables. When there is only one predictor variable and one criterion variable, the procedure is known as *simple regression.*

Chi Square

Chi Square is a statistical test that can be used to analyze results from categorical variables. Categorical variables are variables that contain clearly different groups. The chi-square statistic is used with frequency data. The chi-square value is reported with a probability (p) value indicating significance. For example, we can use chi-square to test for an association between frequency of attendance at organizational meetings and age groups (category variable). Common measures of effect size associated with chi-square analyses are Cramer's V or the phi coefficient.

Reading Complex Research Results

MANOVA

MANOVA is the abbreviation for *Multivariate Analysis of Variance.* The *M* stands for multivariate and refers to the presence of more than one dependent variable. A MANOVA may have one or more independent variables and two or more dependent variables. For example, we could examine the effects of different presenters and different forgiveness programs on forgiveness and compassion. Studies with three to four independent variables and three to four dependent variables can be difficult to interpret because many interactions are possible.

MANCOVA
MANCOVA is a MANOVA procedure that includes one or more covariates. For example, we could examine the effects of different presenters and different motivational programs on measures of optimism and well-being when adjusting for the covariate of age. As with ANCOVA, MANCOVA analyses can include several covariates.

Factor Analysis
Factor analysis is a statistical strategy using correlations to discover patterns of relationships among many variables in a large database. For example, in forgiveness studies, the factors of anger and desire for revenge appear to be linked to the larger concept of forgiveness. There are different types of factor analysis. One common type is called *Principle Components Analysis*.

Multiple Regression
Multiple regression refers to regression procedures in which several predictor variables are used to predict values on one variable. Sometimes the predictor variables are referred to as *independent* variables or *explanatory* variables. Sometimes the variable that is predicted is called a *dependent* variable, *criterion* variable, or *outcome* variable.

Multiple regression is useful in program evaluation research. For example, educational and treatment programs ought to produce outcomes consistent with their stated purposes and goals, such as enriching marriages or reducing alcohol abuse. Surveys may be used to measure outcomes in workshop- and other program-evaluation studies.

Logistic Regression

Logistic regression is used when researchers want to predict an outcome that has two or more categories. They may include several predictors that are either categorical or continuous variables. Suppose surveys were completed about a proposed program. The survey contains items identifying preferences along with person factors like age and gender. The survey also asks respondents to choose one of two program preferences, which we can call *A* or *B*. Logistic regression could be used to predict the likelihood of preferring program A or program B based on a set of predictor variables included in the survey. Instead of predicting a numerical value on the criterion variable as in multiple regression, logistic regression reports the likelihood of the occurrence of one choice or the other. The researchers report an odds ratio—the odds of program choice A or program choice B.

Discriminant Function Analysis

Researchers use *Discriminant Function Analysis* to identify the relative contribution of variables to predict an outcome. The researchers can identify the predictive value of variables alone or in combination with other variables. The outcome variable is a categorical variable. For example, we may want to determine the contribution of different factors linked to success following completion of a community-based substance treatment program. We could define *success* as remaining free of substances for six-months—the outcome variable is either successful or not successful.

Structural Equation Modeling

Structural equation modeling, known as *SEM*, is a complex approach to testing relationships among variables in a theoretical model. Researchers design a visual representation of a model containing variables with lines drawn from one variable to another to indicate hypothesized relationships. Survey data are obtained to test how well the proposed model fits the actual data.

Summary

Reading survey research involves several skills.

Reputable research sources can be found in a web search when you know a particular source. Databases may be the best sources of research and can be accessed through library systems.

Research articles have a common format with the following sections: abstract, introduction with literature review, method, results, discussion, and references.

Reading results can be a challenge because some include complex statistical analyses. The sections usually include descriptive statistics and correlations followed by the analyses linked to hypotheses. Analyzing effect sizes is becoming more important.

Concepts

Abstract-article	Literature review section
ANOVA	Logistic regression

ANCOVA

Chi-square

Correlations

Covariate

Cramer's V

Descriptive Statistics Discriminant function analysis

Discussion section

Effect size

Factor analysis

Hypotheses

Introduction to article

MANOVA

MANCOVA

Method section

Multiple regression

Regression

Results section

Pearson *r*

Phi coefficient

Structural equation modeling

t test

Variable

3. Writing Items and Questions

Objectives:
>   Identify two ways to add items to surveys.
>   Identify advantages and disadvantages of closed- and open-ended items.
>   Identify recommendations for writing different kinds of items.

There are two basic ways to add items to surveys. We can write them ourselves and, with permission, we can include items written by others.

What's the difference between items and questions?

Any statement or question in a survey that prompts people to respond is an item. An item may be either a statement or a question. In addition to questions like "What is your age?", items can be written as statements that prompt respondents to fill in a blank or select an option. For example, instead of asking a question about age, the age item might simply state: "Select your age." This is followed by a list of ages, age groups, or may even be rephrased to request a birth year in programs that automatically calculate age.

What are the two major types of items in surveys?

Two major types of items are called *closed* and *open*. Closed items limit respondents to a few selections. Here's an example of a closed item:

> My life is full of meaning.
>   Strongly agree
>   Agree
>   Disagree

Strongly disagree
Here's an example of an open item:

Please complete the sentence:
"I think of my life as _____."

How can you decide between closed and open items?
There are advantages and disadvantages to closed and open items. Following are some factors to consider when making a decision.

Culture
In some cultures, limiting people to closed, multiple choice style items, seems strange. If most people in a culture prefer to answer open-ended questions, then that may be the best type of item to include. Alternatively, a mix of open and closed items may be best. When thinking about cultural diversity, consider that some people have particular concerns about sharing personal information with the public, responding to people perceived as strangers, using certain methods of technology, and so forth.

Scoring
It is easier to quickly score multiple-choice items as people respond to an online survey. By the time a respondent has completed the survey, the items have been scored and added to the growing database. In contrast, scoring open-ended items requires time to consider how to categorize responses and whether an assignment of numerical values makes sense. Items leading to short answers may be easier to score but may lack richness, which is often the point of answering an open-ended question.

Writing
It can be easier to ask an open-ended question, but like any question—closed or open—precise wording is needed to yield a useful response. In contrast, it takes longer to write a closed item having a few reasonable options. All of the options need to fit the item stem and capture most of the plausible responses. Writing good items often requires pretesting the items on a small sample and replacing or rewriting them based on feedback.

History
Some items have a track record, which can be found by reading journal articles. If items are copyrighted, it may be possible to obtain permission to use them. Items that have performed well in the past may not work well with your sample, but if your sample is similar to those in other studies, you may save considerable time by using the same item set.

What are some guidelines for writing items?
Multiple-choice items are composed of two parts: a stem and a set of responses. The stem is usually a short statement, but it may be a question. The responses are four to five words or phrases that answer the question, complete a sentence, or provide another meaningful response to the stem.

Meaningfulness
All items in a survey should make sense to the participant because they are related to other items and to the overall purpose of the survey. If your survey is about a program to help young mothers, then all the items ought to have something to do with the program even though they may be about a variety of things,

such as cost, time, location, medication, breast feeding, or employment.

Readability

All items should be edited for spelling, punctuation, and grammar. In addition, the reading level should be appropriate for the educational level of the respondents. Avoid professional jargon and most abbreviations unless you are evaluating the respondents' knowledge of specific vocabulary or abbreviations.

Abstract

Asking about values and interests in the abstract can produce answers that are not very useful. Instead, try to ask a question in a specific way. Here are two examples of items that would be followed by a rating scale:

> **Abstract**: How well did you like the "Safe at Home" program?

> **Specific**: How strongly would you recommend the "Safe at Home" program?

Learning how well a respondent liked a program may provide an organization with a general idea, but asking people about their likelihood of recommending the program can help determine a level of liking that involves a personal commitment.

Bias

Avoid words and phrases that imply a negative or positive attitude within a culture. People react emotionally to certain words and phrases. Words in common use a few decades ago can change their meaning and remind people of negative experiences.

For example, if you add the title *Dr.* to a person's name, you add an element of credibility that may increase a speaker's positive rating, making it higher than if you just used their name. If you add the word *liberal* to a program, you may create a negative bias among conservative respondents and a positive bias among those who identify with liberal views. Biases may be hard to identify, so it is a good idea to have your items reviewed by a few people outside the group of people who are writing the items.

Personal

Avoid asking questions that are too personal. Many people object to providing information about their income and sexual behavior. If personal items are important to the survey, consider ways to limit intrusiveness.

For example, people may be asked to report income in categories and given the option of skipping the item. If questions about sex are important, be sure to disclose that such questions will be asked before they take the survey, and permit people to skip items or leave the survey if they feel uncomfortable.

Avoid: How much did you earn last year? _____

Consider: Which category best describes the income you expect to earn this year?
Less than $25,000
Between $25,001 and $50,000
Between $50,001 and $75,000

Modify values as appropriate to your sample.

Ambiguity

Items should be unambiguous. Ambiguous items can produce confusion if respondents feel the answer is sometimes *yes* and sometimes *no* or both *agree* and *disagree* at the same time. Some items cause respondents to think their answer depends on other things you did not include.

For example, consider a situation in which organizations have failed in their attempts to increase income but must balance their budget. They might ask the membership for input using a survey.

> **Ambiguous**: Should we balance our budget by reducing support for community services?

> **Specific**: Which of the following budget items should be reduced to balance the budget? (Provide a list of budget items and offer a write-in item.)

How can we use numbers for categories and ratings?

Some items ask respondents to provide ratings, which result in numbers. The numbers may be present on the rating form, or the numbers may be assigned to responses when they are scored.

For example, questions about educational achievement can list a few categories with an *other* option. And each category can be assigned a number for use in computer-generated reports.

What is the highest level of education you have completed?

Some high school	1
High school	2
Some college	3
College graduate	4
Master's degree	5
Doctorate	6
Other	7

In the educational level example, the numbers only represent categories that will allow for analyses, such as how many people hold similar beliefs depending on their level of education. The numbers may not be visible to the respondent in an online survey application. The options allow for respondents to indicate their level of achievement that has not yet resulted in a diploma or degree. The *other* category allows respondents to enter a unique response.

We can ask people to rate items based on a range of values. The range may use words or numbers. The words representing a range of options may be scored after the survey has been completed. Many items ask people to rate a belief or practice on a five-, seven-, or ten-point scale. For example, we can ask people about the other person in a close relationship. You can substitute an appropriate word for the other person, such as *spouse, partner,* or *friend.*

How close did you feel toward your friend in the past week?
    Very close
    Somewhat close
    In between
    Somewhat distant
    Very distant

In this example, we could assign the number 5 to *very close* and the number 1 to *very distant,* but the participant would not see the numbers when taking the survey. The item could be expanded to use a seven-point rating. Following is an example of a simple 10-point rating scale:

> Please rate the conference dinner on the following items using a 10-point scale where 10 = Excellent and 1 = Poor:
> Presentation of food
> Variety of meal options
> Variety of drink options
> Friendliness of servers

Some numerical scales represent increasing values but look like categories. For example, we may want to assess the frequency of spiritual practices like reading one's sacred text. Each response will be assigned a numerical value after the participant answers the question. Here's an example we might ask of Christians:

How often do you read the Bible?

Daily	6
Almost every day	5
A few days each week	4
At least once a week	3
Several times a month	2
At least once a month	1
Other	0

Some presentations allow respondents to rate items on a 100-point scale using a visual slider or dial. When reporting percentages makes sense, researchers can use 100-point scales. Following are some examples of percentage items:

Use a scale from 0% to 100% when answering the following questions:

- What percentage of the time are you able to find a parking place within 10 minutes of arriving for the meeting?
- What percentage of the time do you take notes during the lecture?

What are some response options?

Following are some examples of options you can use when giving respondents a range of answers to select when rating different types of items. The terms at the end of the range are called *anchors*. Sometimes anchors like *strongly agree* to *strongly disagree* are placed at the ends of a scale, and the in-between words like *agree* or *disagree* are omitted and replaced by numbers or even spaces to represent in-between values. For example, we could ask about overall satisfaction with a work-shop using a 10-point scale that just includes the anchors 1 = *very dissatisfied* to 10 = *very satisfied*.

Satisfaction ratings
Very satisfied
Satisfied
Neutral
Dissatisfied
Very dissatisfied

Agreement ratings
    Strongly agree
    Agree
    Neither agree nor disagree
    Disagree
    Strongly disagree

Importance ratings
    Extremely important
    Very important
    Moderately important
    Slightly important
    Not at all important

Likelihood ratings
    Extremely likely
    Moderately likely
    Slightly likely
    Neither likely or unlikely
    Slightly unlikely
    Moderately unlikely
    Extremely unlikely

What are some guidelines for writing open-ended items?
Open-ended questions allow respondents freedom of expression. No matter how well we construct a survey, we are unlikely to capture everything of importance on a topic. Open-ended questions allow respondents to share their knowledge, opinions, and concerns. Open-ended questions communicate how much you value the contribution of the respondents who have taken their time to answer your questions.

Too many open-ended questions can make it difficult to organize results from large samples. They increase the time it takes to complete a survey and may result in high numbers of incomplete surveys.

When asking several open-ended questions, ask questions that can easily be answered in one or a few words. For example:

- What is your ethnic identity?
- Name three books you would like to discuss in a book study group.
- Where did you meet your spouse?
- What was the most interesting presentation during the conference?
- What did you like least about the workshop?
- How could the seminar be improved?
- What presentations would you like to see added to our annual conference?

How can you obtain items written by others?
If you are conducting research, you will find many items, short scales, and questionnaires online. Some of these items or scales are in research articles. You can usually obtain permission by sending an email to the authors. You should briefly state the purpose of your project and provide contact information for yourself and your organization. When writing the results, be sure to report the name of the scale and list the reference. Keep a copy of the permission response in your project file.

There are several advantages to using published items. In addition to saving time, you can see how well the items worked in similar research. You may also find that someone else thought about related items that you or your team did not consider. Sometimes you may wish to modify an item. If you do, be sure to disclose the modification when presenting the results of your survey.

The International Personality Item Pool (IPIP) is an example of a large source of items dealing with various aspects of personality. There are more than 3,000 items in the database; however, it is important to be careful in selecting the items. The authors recommend you have university coursework in psychological assessment. The authors also explicitly state: "Please don't ask permission." You should still provide the reference source for any of the scales for which references are available. If you do not have the required expertise, consider adding a knowledgeable consultant to your project.

The scales on the IPIP website are organized alphabetically. A few examples include the following:

Compassion
Empathy
Forgiveness
Gratitude
Honesty
Joyfulness
Kindness
Leadership

An Example

Jennifer Pop and her colleagues (2009) wrote and revised survey items to assess a moral response toward clergy who committed a moral failure. They borrowed items from a previous study, used them in a small sample, then, based on feedback, revised the items for her project. Following is a quote from her article.

> All items were seven-point Likert-type items (1 = very strongly disagree, 7 = very strongly agree). Four Restoration to Ministry (RM) items (alpha = 0.61) addressed general attitudes toward restoration. For example, "This pastor should be restored to a similar ministry position with supervision." Three items (alpha = 0.93) focused the participants on Forgiveness and Restoration (FR) and the impact on a victim. An example of an FR item is: "The victim or victims offended by the pastor need to forgive the pastor before the pastor can be restored to the same public ministry position." Finally, we used a one item, Global Restoration Scale (GRS). This was a 10-point measure (1 = no restoration to any public or nonpublic ministry, 10 = full restoration to the same public ministry). All participants completed a background questionnaire that assessed age, gender, and ethnicity. (p. 289)

In reading the article text, notice that the survey was rather short even though she measured different kinds of responses to the problem scenario. She refers to *Likert-type* items. Items that provide a range of options like *strongly disagree* to *strongly agree* are sometimes referred to as *Likert-type scales* after the psychologist Rensis Likert, who invented the type of scale. Sometimes they are just called *rating scales*. Also notice the use of a one-item scale rated as one to ten. And finally, notice that at the end of her survey she collected the social-context information of age, gender, and ethnicity. Because she did this, she was able to adjust the results for gender, which was needed because most people were women.

Summary

Survey items can be statements or questions.

Closed items limit respondents to a few options. Open items allow respondents to enter their thoughts.

Closed items are easy to score but may not fit well with all cultures. They may also require more time to create than an open-ended question.

Open items are usually easier to write than closed items, but they often take longer to score—especially when the answers are lengthy.

Write items that are meaningful, readable, unambiguous, specific, unbiased, and not too personal.

Numbers can be used to identify items presented as categories, like education level, geographic region, and ethnicity.

Numbers can also be assigned to words and phrases that indicate a range of values in response to a statement. Many scales use a range of 5 to 7 points, but some slider scales can range from 0 to 100 when referring to percentages.

Many survey items ask respondents to rate items using anchor words and phrases to address satisfaction, agreement, or importance.

Guidelines specific to open-ended questions include considering respondents time to respond to items and researcher's time to write and score items. It is best when most items only require a brief response.

It is possible to use survey items written by others. Many are free to use in research and teaching by just including the reference when writing reports. If permission is not explicitly granted, contact the author or publisher for permission.

Many test publishers maintain strict control over their items; thus, they are not available for inclusion in surveys.

Concepts
Anchors
Closed-ended items
Likert-type scale
Open-ended items

4. Organizing and Formatting Surveys

Objectives:
>Identify factors related to survey length and time.
>Identify suggestions for the order of items in a survey.
>Identify considerations when administering surveys during an interview.

Survey Length and Time

Respondents complete surveys at different rates depending on several factors, including motivation, item complexity, number of items, and overall length of the survey. Obviously, the more items included in a survey, the longer the survey, but more difficult items and the length of instructions can increase the time it takes to complete a survey.

Deciding on survey length and time involves a consideration of several factors, which may only be known by conducting a trial and asking for feedback in addition to calculating the time it takes to complete the survey. Respondents can often complete two to three items per minute, but again, item difficulty and the overall length of the survey will make a difference.

Item Order

Early items should be obviously relevant to the purpose of the survey from the respondent's perspective rather than the research team's. Although researchers may have good reasons to ask questions less obviously related to a topic, if respondents do not perceive early items as relevant to the stated purpose of the survey, their motivation can be reduced. Therefore, place items less obviously related to the primary survey topic later in the survey.

Early items should be easier to answer than later items. There are cases when we wish to obtain subjective opinions, which might require some thinking. In general, it is best to place the more subjective or complex items later in a survey.

Omit items that are similar to other items. It can be frustrating to respondents when they feel like they have already answered a question. Thus, unless you have an important reason to repeat an item or ask a similar question a second time, remove duplicate or similar items. If similar items are important to your project, consider telling respondents that they may encounter similar items and explain the purpose of the apparent duplication.

Sequence the order of items by time of events or development. Questions about historical events should be from earlier to more recent times, so 2016 before 2020. Questions about experiences should follow the usual progression of events that occur in elementary school, high school, young adulthood, and so on. Questions about early relationships should occur before questions about more recent relationships.

Sequence the items in a logical manner such that later questions do not cause respondents to wonder about their answers to previous questions. If you ask respondents a simple question about being prolife or prochoice before you ask more nuanced questions about permitting abortion in cases of rape, incest, or saving the physical life of a mother, you may produce frustration in respondents who think carefully about their answers and desire to respond in a consistent manner.

Items likely to be highly personal are best placed later in the survey when the respondent has been prepared for relevant topics based on earlier items. What counts as a sensitive item will vary with respondents but may include opinions about abortion, gun control, capital punishment, finances, and sexuality.

Group items in a logical order based on topic or subtopic. When asking respondents about their spiritual beliefs, religious practices, and attitudes toward various social issues, keep the items together that are relevant to the subtopic. Also, provide a brief transition statement when moving from one subtopic to another.

For example, when my colleagues and I asked Christians about their beliefs, we provided a short introductory question before providing a list of belief statements to be rated on a 5-point scale from 1 = *strongly disagree* to 5 = *strongly agree* (Sutton et al., 2016). Here's the question with two of the items.

What are your personal beliefs?
God heals some people without human intervention.
I have had a born-again experience.

Survey Appearance

Whether presenting a survey online or on paper, check to see how the survey appears to respondents. The better online survey providers will take care of most formatting to ensure a neat and pleasing presentation on various screen sizes such as desktop displays, tablets, and small screens. However, it is important to check for appearance to help respondents attend to the questions rather than a distracting or difficult-to-read presentation.

Items and spacing requirements vary with the screen size. On small screens, there is usually only space for a short item and a few responses. Large screens may accommodate a few items and a 5-point response range. For those using printed forms, ensure there is adequate space for entering written comments and the font size is large enough for most readers.

Branching and skipping strategies are useful when a group of items does not apply to some respondents. However, it is important to ensure that the branching works as planned. When working with Johan Mostert to assess Christian virtues in a young adult version of the *Discipleship Dynamics*^{TM} survey (2015), we placed items relevant to married couples near the end of the survey. We included a branching strategy so that those who were not married ended their survey if they reported their relationship status as anything other than married. Ask your survey provider to explain how to use a branching strategy.

Use of Incentives

Incentives encourage people to complete surveys. Incentives can vary considerably with budget size and audience. Examples of incentives include money, gift cards, coupons, a donation to a charity, and entry into a drawing for a few larger prizes. Experience indicates cash is the most preferred incentive.

The amount of incentive should vary with your audience. Some will be motivated by helping students complete research projects, others are glad to contribute to a meaningful inquiry about a ministry or building project. Some respondents are interested in being part of an investigation, and others are motivated by an opportunity to earn a little extra money. For some $25 is a lot of money. But to those earning $200,000 a year, even $40 is not a lot to interrupt a busy day. Students may be motivated to earn extra credit.

Preparing for Interviews

In this section, I present suggestions on administering a survey in the context of an interview. An interview is a direct method of asking people questions and may be conducted by one or more interviewers asking questions of one person or a group. Interviews can be conducted face-to-face, by phone, or by chat.

Decide on Method

Interviews may be conducted in person with individuals, couples, or small groups. They may also be conducted via electronic communications using chat or audio–video methods. Face-to-face interviews may include responding to questions on an electronic device with or without a recording When selecting a method of presenting items, keep in mind that people are differently abled.

Recruit and Train

Whether your project is simple or complex, it is important that all interviewers receive the same training so the survey is delivered in the same way. Best results are usually obtained when the interviewer is from the same culture as the respondent. Consider the interviewer's accent and pronunciation when matching interviewers to respondents. Clothes, tattoos, hairstyles, and other aspects of appearance of interviewers should be within cultural norms for what respondents consider trustworthy, acceptable, and not distracting.

Provide an opportunity for interviewers to ask questions during training and via calls or messages during the administration of the interview. For long-term projects, you may need to meet more than once to ensure interviewers continue to follow the same presentation of greetings, instructions, and questions.

Instruct interviewers on methods for people who are differently abled. Electronic devices include technologies to accommodate different audio and visual presentations and methods of responding. At times, an assistant may be needed.

Support Interviewers
Consider the amount of work you require of your interviewers. To maintain quality control, offer adequate pay or incentives and provide refreshments and breaks during training sessions that last more than 90 minutes.

Prepare Scripts
Scripts guide interviewers throughout an interview. Provide standard language for introductions, answers to common questions, and closing an interview session. If you plan follow-up interviews, provide guidance for those as well.

Organize Practice Sessions
Consistency is critical to obtaining reliable results. Delivering the interview in a consistent manner requires some practice. Plan to observe the practice sessions and provide feedback as needed to ensure all interviewers follow the script. Observing practice sessions is a way to revise the script to include answers to new questions that may arise.

Monitor Interviews
Plan to monitor interviews at least on a random basis to ensure the surveys are administered according to the script. Monitoring may be done via recordings or by accompanying the interviewer.

Check Technology

Ensure that all technological devices are in good working order and that you can access technical assistance as needed.

Test the survey before going public. Plan on a few trials to ensure the survey provides the data you planned to obtain. An early trial with the research team and a few friends can help identify and correct simple problems of content and method. Before going public, conduct a trial run with a small sample of people who are similar to your intended audience. Ask for feedback and make necessary corrections. Testing can prevent wasting the time of respondents and project team members.

Summary

The length of a survey varies with the length of instructions, the number of items, the length of the items, and the number of options per item or text space associated with open-ended items.

The time to complete a survey depends on the length as well as the complexity of the instructions and items.

Although most people can complete two to three multiple choice items per minute, item difficulty and overall length as well as individual variability can affect total response time. A trial is needed to calculate an average response time.

Item order is important. It is best to begin with items obviously relevant to the topic as well as those easy to answer. Place less obvious and more difficult items toward the end of a survey.

Order items logically. For example, order older dates before more recent dates. Ask questions about early ages or grades before more recent ones.

Avoid asking questions that may produce frustration because responding to a current item would produce a desire to change a response to a previous item.

It is usually best to place highly sensitive items later in a survey, but it is still important to disclose the fact that the survey includes sensitive items.

When there are different groups of items, provide a transition statement.

Check the layout of a survey—especially when presenting it in different formats. Lengthy items may be difficult to read on small screens.

Incentives can encourage task completion.

Surveys can be administered during an interview. Interviewers should be sensitive to the culture of the respondents and participate in organized practice sessions using scripts. Interviewers should be supervised and the interviews monitored for quality assurance.

Check that all technology works before administering a survey.

Concepts

Branching strategy
Incentives
Interview
Script

5. Getting Approval: Ethical Thinking

Objectives:
   Identify the role of the review board in research.
   Identify common elements associated with the concept *informed consent.*
   Identify ethical procedures before, during, and following survey administration.

You will need to know the ethical principles and laws applicable to the location where you plan to administer your survey. Ethical principles vary with the professions; however, in general, ethical principles and laws exist to protect people's privacy and well-being. Fortunately, many surveys involve minimal risk and are therefore easily approved, but a review by an external team is important and in many cases mandatory. Universities, hospitals, and research organizations have research policies that define risk and describe research review procedures. You will find links to the ethical standards of various professions in appendix B. I recommend you obtain a copy for your profession.

Review Boards

Before conducting your survey, you will need to obtain approval from a research review board, sometimes referred to as an *IRB* (Institutional Review Board). Each organization will have guidelines and forms to complete for your project to be reviewed. In the United States, most surveys are considered research projects that require review board approval.

If you are working with people in different locations, other review boards will need to be involved. For example, if you are in a university graduate program and have team members who work for a hospital and another university, all of the re-view boards will need to approve the project. Review board approval is required before beginning trials and "pretesting" of the survey.

If you are a member of a professional association, check their guidelines on the ethical conduct of research. Follow re-porting requirements if respondents disclose information that must be reported. For example, many professionals in the United States are required to report intent to harm oneself or others. Interviewers should have information on emergency hotlines and crisis intervention centers.

Informed Consent

Following approval, respondents should be able to give in-formed consent before taking the survey. Informed consent will vary with laws and regulations, so be sure to check with the requirements in your area. Guidelines for informed consent may be available from your government, organization, profes-sional association, or grant source.

Informed consent usually includes the items in the list that follows. See appendix C for an example of an informed con-sent statement.

Statement. A statement using the words "Informed Consent to Participate in a Survey"

Title. Display the title of the survey.

Age. State the appropriate age range. Keep in mind the age of consent in your location. For example, in the United States, the usual age of consent is 18. Parents or legal guardians must be contacted to provide consent for those underage or having a legal guardian. The rights of children and those having a guardian must be respected; thus, even though they cannot provide legal consent, they have the right of assent to or dissent from participation in a survey.

Purpose. Write a sentence that clearly states the purpose of the survey.

Procedures. State the procedures involved in taking the survey, including an estimate of how much time it takes to complete the survey.

Risks. Disclose any potential risks or discomforts in taking the survey. Consider whether the risks are about the same as those encountered in daily life. Consider whether there are personal items that some respondents might find embarrassing, distressing, or disturbing. Questions about sexual behavior or abuse, substance use, and crime can be disturbing or pose a risk. If your survey is part of a research project, clearly state any procedures that are experimental.

Benefits. Identify potential benefits of taking the survey. Consider how the respondent or society may be improved as a result of the information obtained.

Payments or incentives. Disclose what will be paid to the respondent. If there are no payments or incentives, state this fact.

Confidentiality statement. Describe how you will maintain confidentiality. State how results will be disclosed. For example, presenting a summary at a meeting or in a publication.

Withdrawal procedure. State that participation is voluntary. State that a respondent can withdraw from the survey at any time without penalty or loss of benefits. Describe how they can leave a survey—for example, by closing their browser.

Contacts. Identify the person or persons to be contacted if there are any questions. Include the method of contact, such as a phone number and email.

After the Survey

At the end of a survey, it is customary to provide a debriefing statement in which you explain the purpose of the survey and thank the participants. See appendix D for an example of a debriefing statement. After the data are collected, ensure that the privacy of all respondents is respected. Remove any personally identifying information from the database and use a code for the individual respondents rather than a name, email, or other personal identification such as an IP address. Ensure that the data are stored on a secure server and that back-up procedures maintain the integrity of the data.

Other Notes

Ensure that all people involved in conducting your study have completed instruction on the protection of human subjects in research projects.

Avoid interviewing people who are driving or operating heavy equipment.

Administrators are sometimes contacted for permission to allow researchers to conduct a survey in their organization. The checklist in appendix A may help you with items to consider when you review such requests.

See appendix B for a list of websites where you can find information on ethical principles.

Summary

Before administering a survey, know the ethical principles and laws applicable to the location where the survey will be administered. In general, ethical principles and laws exist to protect people's privacy and well-being.

Many surveys involve minimal risk but still require approval by a research review board. Universities, hospitals, and research organizations have research policies that define risk and describe research review procedures.

Ethical procedures must be followed before, during, and following the survey process.

Concepts
Confidentiality
Debriefing
Incentives
Institutional Review Board

6. Selecting Respondents

Objectives:
>Identify different sampling methods.
>Identify factors to consider when sampling.

Obtaining Samples

Most local and student research projects depend on convenience samples, which are composed of volunteers who are easily recruited and available. In this section, I will review information about sampling strategies.

Any consideration of sampling begins with an understanding of the population from which we wish to obtain a sample. As you might guess, obtaining a sizeable sample from a national population is an expensive endeavor usually undertaken by large companies. A population may be defined as all the people in a nation, all the people who identify as part of a religious group, all the people who identify as alumni, and so forth. In short, researchers decide the characteristics of the people in a population. This list is the sampling frame. Once the population has been defined, researchers can select a method to obtain a sample.

Random Samples

Random samples are usually the best way to avoid bias produced by nonrandom methods. Random sampling aims to avoid bias by using statistical procedures to ensure everyone in a population has an equal chance of being included in a survey. Unfortunately, this is not easy to carry out in a large population. In a small population, each person can be assigned a number. Information from a software program or table of random numbers can be used to generate a list of numbers to include in the survey sample. For example, to sample 200 students from a population of 2,500, we would need to generate 200 random numbers and select those students whose assigned number matches the numbers from the randomly generated list.

Stratified Random Samples

In some cases, we want to ensure that people with specific characteristics are included in a survey. If we know that 40% of leaders in a population are women and 25% are African American, then we can subdivide the population into groups based on gender and ethnicity. After the subgroups are formed, we randomly select people from those groups. In the language of research, the subgroups are referred to as *strata,* and the method is called *stratified random sampling.* With large populations, researchers can include many strata. For example, you can form groups based on geographic location, gender, ethnicity, age, and belief.

Cluster Samples

If you were conducting a random sample of students in colleges and universities, it may be inefficient to pick a few students from each of more than 100 schools. Instead, you might consider cluster sampling. Cluster sampling can be random or stratified. A cluster may consist of all the students in a college. Colleges can be identified by number. All the students in colleges selected by a random number generator will be sampled.

Alternatively, if you want to ensure certain characteristics of a population are present in the clusters, a *stratified random cluster* method can be used. For example, if a researcher wanted to sample people in different-size congregations who attend churches located in different geographic regions, researchers would form subgroups based on the criteria of congregation size and location. Then researchers would randomly sample all congregants attending a church that met the criteria. Using these twin criteria of congregation size and region, you might first decide on how many subgroups of what size make sense for your study. An example could be small, medium, and large congregations where you specify how many people fit those size categories. Next you need to decide on regions. In the United States, the census uses nine regions (www.census.gov).

Systematic Samples

A systematic sampling method is sometimes useful. To obtain a sample of 100 people from a population of 700, you could randomly pick a number from 1 to 6 as your starting person in the list of 700. Suppose you selected person number 5. You would then go down the list picking every 6th person after person 5 until you selected 100 people. This can work unless you have reason to believe the order of your list contains some bias. The systematic sampling method can be used to select classrooms, congregations, and other subgroups when using a cluster method. You will need rules to handle situations when people are unavailable. For example, randomly selecting a second time to complete the goal of 100 people.

Convenience Samples

Convenience samples are common in many settings. Convenience samples are composed of people who are available and willing to complete the survey. However, convenience samples may be biased in many unknown ways. For example, convenience samples may exclude those who are unavailable because of employment, unwilling to disclose personal information, or have a particular agenda or complaint, and so forth. If you know of possible ways convenience samples may differ from those who are not available, you may ask questions to discern those key characteristics such as age, employment, complaints, and so forth.

Other ways to obtain convenience samples include snowball, quota, focus groups, and panels. *Snowball* or *referral samples* begin with an available sample, such as known college presidents, then those respondents are asked to nominate other presidents for inclusion. In *quota samples*, researchers form subgroups based on specific percentages of people who have characteristics they want to include. This is like a stratified sample but may not be obtained by randomization.

Focus Groups and Panels
Focus groups are small groups brought together because they are thought to represent some important aspect of a population. For example, to consider the impact of a project on a congregation, a focus group may be formed of 15 to 20 people who represent different interests in a congregation or organization. A leader then asks questions of the group. One or more assistants usually record the meeting and take notes. In addition to presenting questions to the group, the focus group leader might ask participants to complete a short survey containing closed-end questions.

Panels, like focus groups, are formed of people representing a specific population. For example, they may have expertise related to a program or building project. Respondents may be recruited to help make decisions about new programs or problems to be resolved. Again, experienced leaders and assistants are needed to collect and organize the information so the group leader can remain on script and guide the discussion.

Sample Size

How large should a sample be? As with many things in life, the answer to sample size is "it all depends." If you are using a survey to collect opinions from employees or members of a congregation, then you might send a broadcast message or email to all persons followed by a reminder after two weeks and again at four weeks. Although you are interested in everyone's opinion, you cannot force people to volunteer. The situation is similar for faculty and students at a college or university.

If you are conducting a survey following the presentation of a workshop or other educational program, you will likely try to get feedback from everyone who attended. The ideal time is usually at the close of the workshop. Once again, you will send follow-up requests, then close the survey and analyze the available results at specified dates.

In contrast, if you are planning to obtain a representative sample from a large population, you will probably want to consider how large a sample you need to draw conclusions about the entire population. To consider sample size, you need to know the answer to a few questions, which involves learning new concepts: *confidence interval* and *confidence level*. These two concepts are related to the concept of *sampling error*.

All statistics calculated on samples are imprecise—they contain error. Researchers are able to estimate the amount of sampling error. The larger the sample, the less error is involved in the estimate of the population values. You have probably seen polling results reported in terms of a percentage of people who are likely to vote for a particular candidate. In addition to the percentage, the results usually include a margin of error. For example, 45% (+/- 3%) say they will vote for candidate Lopez. The confidence interval is the range above and below the reported value. In the example, the confidence interval is 42% to 48%.

The confidence level tells you how likely the researcher thinks the population value will fall within the confidence interval. A common level of confidence is 95%, but you will sometimes see 99% in research projects.

Your statistician will be able to calculate the sample size you will need if you provide the consultant with three pieces of information: population size, confidence level, and confidence interval. If you are dealing with a very large population, you can skip the population size because at very large numbers, sample sizes of 1,000 are usually adequate. Following are some examples of sample sizes recommended for different populations using a confidence level of 95% and a confidence interval of 3%:

Population size	Confidence level	Confidence Interval	Sample size needed
100,000	95%	3%	1056
10,000	95%	3%	964
1,000	95%	3%	516
500	95%	3%	341
250	95%	3%	203

Translating Surveys
Translating surveys from one language to another is not a simple task because there are nuances that would only be known

to someone fluent in the two languages under consideration. Thus, the first task is to locate a speaker fluent in the two languages and the relevant cultures.

After a survey has been translated, feedback should be obtained by native speakers in the new language to ensure the new wording matches the original intent. Use the feedback to make revisions.

The next step is to hire a new translator to translate the survey from the new language back to the original language. Check to see if this "back-translation" version is true to the original. If not, work with the translators on another revision. Retest the survey on another small sample. Use their feedback to make any final revisions.

When asking about race or ethnicity, consider using categories common to government census surveys where your sample resides. Keep in mind that sign languages are not the same as spoken languages (see for example Swisher, 1988).

An Example

Because most premarital education is done by clergy, Joe Wilmoth and Susan Smyser (2012) of Mississippi State wanted to discover how clergy prepared couples for marriage. Based on data indicating the largest religious groups, they used a stratified random sampling method. This method resulted in identifying 2,000 congregations. They then contacted the clergy to complete their four-page 126-item survey. They ended up with 820 responses, 793 of which were usable.

Several points are worth summarizing because they may apply to other studies. Wilmoth and Smyser began with a very practical goal of identifying the practices of most people who provide premarital education. Because they discovered most premarital education was performed by clergy, they were able to locate a resource to help them define their population. Even though less than half of their surveys were returned, they still ended up with a large sample size. It's clearly good to remember that despite contacting a large number of potential respondents, your response rate will usually be less than half of the original number. If you have the time, I recommend you read the article to learn more about the survey process.

Additional Chapter Notes

World surveys and government census data provide examples of how governments examine the characteristics of their population in terms of specific subgroups. See the following links for a few examples.

Canada: www.statcan.gc.ca

United Kingdom: http://www.nationalarchives.gov.uk/

United States: www.census.gov

International Census Programs: https://www.census.gov/population/international/about/index.html

You may also find the World Values Survey of interest: http://www.worldvaluessurvey.org/

Summary

There are several ways to obtain a sample. Researchers begin by defining a population then decide how they will select a sample.

Random samples are usually the best method. Stratified random sampling can ensure that members of important subgroups are included in a sample. A truly random sample may omit representatives from different subgroups that should be included.

Consider cluster sampling when you wish to sample people who are members of groups like colleges, churches, or other organizations. Clusters can also be stratified.

Many projects include convenience samples, which can be subject to unknown biases unless you ask questions to identify specific characteristics relevant to the project.

Focus groups and panels may be appropriate when in-depth opinions are sought from a group of experts.

Decisions about sample size depend on several factors including the size of the population as well as statistical factors. You will need to provide your statistical consultant with an estimate of population size, confidence level, and confidence interval to obtain an estimate of an adequate sample size. A sample of 1,000 people is often an adequate sample of very large populations.

Note that translating a survey into a foreign language is not just about translating words. Translators must be fluent in the language of the original and new languages considered.

Concepts

Cluster sample	Referral sample
Confidence interval	Sample
Confidence level	Sampling error
Convenience sample	Sampling frame
Focus group	Snowball sample
Panel	Strata

Population   Stratified cluster sample
Quota sample   Stratified random sample
Random sample   Systematic sample

Part II:

Using Surveys to Understand People

7. Considering Multiple Dimensions

Objectives:

>Identify different types of information that can be obtained from a survey using the SCOPES model.
>
>Describe six dimensions of human functioning according to the SCOPES model.
>
>Identify factors to consider when drawing conclusions from descriptive surveys.

Surveys include questions to understand something about the people who answered the questions. Many surveys ask only a few questions, such as age, sex, location, and employment, in addition to collecting opinions or other information such as attitudes or practices. My aim in this chapter is to present a broad overview of what we can assess with a survey. Specifically, I will present six dimensions of human nature commonly discussed in behavioral science literature: social context, cognition or thinking, behavior or personality, physiology and health status, emotion or feelings, and spirituality. To one degree or another, each dimension of ourselves affects other dimensions. It is hard to think, experience joy, and meet with others when in serious pain. When we are with someone we love in a romantic setting, we may feel fantastic, think only good thoughts, and ignore at least minor ailments. I have created the acronym *SCOPES* to help remember these six dimensions. Finally, I will close the chapter with a section on drawing conclusions.

In a descriptive study, we simply administer a survey to a group of people. If we group people by age it is sometimes called a *cross-sectional research design*. The information can be used to plan new programs and services or modify existing programs and services. We can also gather information related to facilities, such as building projects, parking lot expansions, and so on. The kind of information we obtain will vary according to the answers we need. It is important to decide what kinds of information we want to obtain, which is the point of the next section covering six major dimensions of human functioning.

Overview of the SCOPES Model

The SCOPES model is my organization and expansion of common ways to think about people. Although many researchers refer to various aspects of human functioning when writing textbooks on psychology, few group the functioning into a coherent multidimensional view. One early theorist to create a multidimensional approach was Arnold Lazarus (1989), who developed a seven-component, multimodal model focused on mental health treatment. Other theorists have emphasized the importance of various dimensions or grouping of dimensions. In this section, we will look at six dimensions forming the acronym *SCOPES*: Social context (people, places, time), Cognition (thoughts, beliefs, opinions, problem-solving, memory), Observed behavior patterns or personality, Physiology (factors related to health and our biological functioning), Emotions or feelings, and Spirituality, which may include traditional religious affiliation and those unique ways people combine beliefs, practices, and experiences into a meaningful life.

We all function in a social context characterized by people, places, and time. Within our social spaces, relationships are often critical to understanding who we are and how we function at home, school, work, or in the community. My thinking about our social space was influenced by Kurt Lewin, whose *field theory* proposed that behavior was a function of a person and their environment (Burnes & Cooke, 2013). Psychology students learn about the ABCs: *affect, behavior,* and *cognition.* The three terms represent a core of individual functioning within social space. Researchers continue to explore the interrelationships among the three core variables (e.g., Farley & Stasson, 2003) and relationships to other variables, such as attitudes toward groups (e.g., Jackson et al., 1996), and links to personality (e.g., Wilt & Revelle, 2015). Behavioral health research continues to identify interactions between physical well-being and other aspects of functioning. This interaction, sometimes referred to as *biopsychology, biosociology,* or *biopsychosocial factors,* is not always easy to discern (Miller, 1996). An example of the importance of biopsychosocial factors influencing thoughts, feelings, and behavior may be seen in the recent movement by psychologists to gain prescription privileges (Antonuccio et al., 2003). Finally, spirituality is another dimension of life that has recently gained recognition for its importance to well-being. Assessing spirituality is becoming more common when people seek medical and psychological treatment (D'Souza, 2007). When all six dimensions are considered, the term *theobiopsychosocial model,* though a bit cumbersome, covers the SCOPES model factors.

S Social Context

It's no secret that people are social beings, yet some speak about human behavior as if individuals have no context. As mentioned previously, Lewin studied people in their social context, which he referred to as *lifespace.* Like other researchers (e.g., Burnes & Cooke, 2013), I consider Lewin's core concepts still relevant to understanding how people behave individually as well as in groups and organizations (Sutton, 2016).

In place of the term *lifespace,* I use the term *social context.* Within social context I include people, places, animals, and objects that influence the other five aspects of functioning. People report different feelings and thoughts, including spiritual experiences, when alone on a mountain trail compared to making small talk at an office party, or attending religious services. They will respond differently if they have a headache or recently lost a family member. In addition to these social settings, there is a time component. Each of us experiences a different timeline. We may share similar broad cultural timelines related to floods and wars, similar family timelines related to birthday parties and marriage celebrations. But we also have unique timelines linked to personal achievements, relationships, and meaningful life experiences.

Social context includes that critical aspect of life, relationships. For the most part, people are raised by one or more parents or adult caregivers. Sometimes our relatives are also counted as friends. In addition to family, we have friends throughout life, and some of us have had friends since childhood. Most of us also have romantic relationships. And most people marry at least once. We also have friendships linked to social organizations such as school, work, and places of worship. Relationships are marked by different levels of influence and commitment. We both influence others and are influenced by others.

Social context can be partially identified by various social markers commonly called *demographics*. These items on surveys ask about age, sex, gender, occupation, educational level, military status, relationship status, residence, religious affiliation, political affiliation, hobbies, and so forth. Understanding people includes an understanding of their social context.

C Cognition

People report their thoughts about themselves and others on surveys. Cognition includes visual imagery as well as thoughts we identify as opinions and beliefs. Strongly held beliefs may be combined with emotions and form attitudes, which are predispositions to behave in a certain way. Many surveys deal with what people think, so I will expand this cognition subsection to include subcategories.

Opinions

Opinions represent judgments about a particular event or activity. Opinions are not as strong as beliefs. Think of items that answer the question, "What do people think about___?" Opinion statements could be presented as items to be rated from *strongly agree* to *strongly disagree.*

Beliefs

Beliefs are important thoughts people hold as true about something. Beliefs are stronger than opinions and less likely to change than opinions. Think of items that answer the question, "What do people believe about ___?" Belief statements can also be presented as items to be rated from *strongly agree* to *strongly disagree.*

Attitudes

Attitudes involve thoughts and feelings about acting in a specific way toward an event, activity, or group. An attitude is a predisposition to act. Think of items that answer the question, "What is their attitude toward ___?" We want to detect a tendency to act based on some combination of thoughts and feelings. Statements beginning with the pronoun *I* could be presented as attitude items to be rated from *strongly agree* to *strongly disagree.*

Knowledge

Knowledge consists of facts, concepts, and principles that are generally held to be true by experts in a particular field. Clearly, people can dispute facts, define concepts in different ways, and argue about the applicability of certain principles. Think of items that answer the question, "What do people know about ___?" We could be more precise and ask what facts, concepts, or principles people know.

Facts, concepts, and principles are components of knowledge. Many school tests focus on knowledge of facts, such as who were the founders of a nation or a religion. We can ask for factual knowledge about local laws and organizational policies. And we can ask about facts relevant to knowledge taught in a workshop or other educational program. Facts are simple units of information that most, if not all, experts agree are true.

Concepts are ideas. Concepts are usually explained by definitions along with lists of critical features. Concepts are sometimes taught by pointing to examples and nonexamples. We can learn what inspirational leadership is by seeing examples of such leaders in action contrasted with other types of leadership styles. We could also benefit from someone pointing to the features that are unique to inspirational leadership.

The concepts *Christian, Jew,* and *Muslim* are defined in different ways. We can ask a simple question about faith identity and provide a common list of religious affiliations. We can be more specific to include subgroups of people with identified belief sets, such as Catholic or Methodist. We can attempt to understand how people identify specific aspects of spirituality by asking about their beliefs; for example, we can ask Christians about Jesus' identity as God's son, or whether they agree with points in the Apostle's creed or endorse items from a list of features we expect to be true of someone who identifies as a Christian.

Principles are statements about relationships, which can involve two or more concepts. An example of a simple principle is "round things roll." To understand the principle, we need to understand the concept *round* and the concept *roll*. The teaching, *love your neighbor as yourself* (Mark 12:31) includes the concepts of *love, neighbor,* and *self* and states the relationship between neighbor and self. As you are likely aware, people disagree about the attributes of the concept *love* and what it means to love *as yourself.*

O Observable Behavior Patterns—Personality

Surveys cannot assess actual behavior, but surveys can assess how people describe their behavior patterns. Observable behavior patterns are personality traits that can be identified by other persons. Personality traits are those mostly stable patterns of behavior we use to describe ourselves and others. Some common personality traits known as *The Big Five* include openness, conscientiousness, extroversion, agreeableness, and neuroticism. Understanding people includes an understanding of their behavior patterns or personality traits and the link to thoughts, feelings, spirituality, health, and socialization. Personality traits are important to all of life's relationships.

Some behavior patterns or traits result in conflicts at work, in community organizations, and in the home. You are probably familiar with terms for some of the problematic behavior patterns, such as narcissism and psychopathy. Although these terms make headlines when people with such traits do harm, other personality traits are equally important. For example, Brent Roberts and his colleagues (2007) wrote *The Power of Personality,* in which they found evidence supporting the role of personality traits as predictors of such life events as occupational level, divorce, and mortality.

P   Physiology

We may not notice the effects of our health on our well-being until we feel ill, experience pain, or receive a scary diagnosis. Sometimes a person's health is the focus of a survey, and sometimes it is related to other questions we are asking. Our physical health is a factor related to other dimensions of functioning.

Bodies respond differently to prescribed medication and illegal drugs. Medicines carry side effects, and public service announcements warn of problems with certain drugs. Medicines influence energy levels, thoughts, feelings, behavior, and even spiritual experiences.

Sexual functioning involves external organs as well as neurochemical processes in the brain. Drugs and social setting can affect sexual desire. Sexuality also involves thoughts and feelings. And some report spiritual experiences accompanying sex (see for example Sutton, 2016).

Surveys can only assess what people believe is true about their health. Understanding people includes an understanding of their health and its relationship to thoughts, feelings, behavior, spirituality, and social context.

E   Emotions—Feelings

People feel a lot of things. And the words for emotions vary considerably. Researchers disagree about core emotions, but there is agreement that people evaluate situations differently, which has an effect on their emotional responses. Also, emotions are often linked to behavior in a way that drives action to satisfy needs. Whatever core emotions exist, there are some linked to pleasant mental states we may call happiness and joy. Other emotions linked to unpleasant states include anger, anxiety/fear, sadness/unhappiness, and disgust. To read more about emotions, see *Emotion* by Annett Schirmer (2015). Understanding people includes an understanding of their emotions and the link between emotions, thoughts, behavior patterns, spirituality, health, and socialization.

S   Spirituality—Beliefs, Practices, Experiences

Most people in the world identify with a religion. People of faith hold a variety of beliefs, engage in different practices, and report different experiences. Some of these beliefs, practices, and experiences are common to a particular faith, but others are more personal. On the one hand, people identify with different religions (e.g., Christianity, Judaism, Islam) or groups within a religion (e.g., Christians as Catholics, Anglicans, Methodists), and on the other hand, people have unique beliefs and practices often shaped by their spiritual experiences—people experience God in different ways.

Drawing Conclusions about People

Researchers are never in a position to speak with certainty about results. In addition to the problems of error referred to previously, things happen that can interfere with drawing firm conclusions. Here are a few common problems to keep in mind when attempting to draw conclusions about people from a one-time survey.

People change. People change during a day, a week, or a month. Recent events can influence thoughts, feelings, and behavior. The findings from a one-time survey should not be used to draw conclusions about the past or the future. Some people may be ill or thinking of a pressing family concern when taking the survey. Positive events like the birth of a grandchild, a family wedding, and a promotion at work, can also influence outcomes.

Things happen. Imagine taking a survey about stress in New York City a day following the 9/11 attacks. That is an extreme example, of course. But other things happen as well. Construction noise outside a facility can annoy survey participants. Technology can malfunction, which can affect mood and motivation. Weather events often interfere with our best plans. All things occur within a historical context, and external events can make a difference in how people respond to surveys.

People quit taking surveys. There are many reasons why people fail to complete surveys. Some have to do with the content or the length of the survey, but others have to do with the demands of work and family. We often do not know why people fail to complete surveys. Incomplete surveys can remind us that not everyone is represented in the data we have.

People respond to being studied. Many people change their behavior if they sense they are being watched. Most people want to make a good impression, so their clothes, language, and behavior can change in response to the situation and the people present. This effect, known as the *Hawthorne effect*, is something to be aware of when drawing conclusions about changes attributed to an educational program, ministry or other program when people are completing a one-time survey.

People grow in different ways. Many church ministries, government services, and educational programs are important to a community, but some people change as a result of other activities. For example, some may make life-transforming decisions in response to personal prayer and reading scriptures. Others may respond to a television program or attendance at a special event. We do not always know what survey respondents did outside of the program we intend to evaluate with a one-time survey.

Finally, we should consider that any combination of events and experiences outside our control can make a difference in the lives of people participating in a survey. This should not discourage us from conducting a survey, but it should help us be humble and take a tentative attitude toward any results we obtain, whether they be favorable or unfavorable.

Resource Note

The American Psychological Association (apa.org) maintains a database of tests and measures called *PsycTESTS*. This database includes references to over 40,000 measures—from short surveys containing a few items to research questionnaires with dozens of items. The focus is on research instruments referred to as *measures, scales,* or *surveys* in a wide variety of fields such as the behavioral and social sciences and education. As the information indicates, the database can help you conduct or create research without having to reinvent the wheel. In my experience, the measures provide some sense of what works and what does not work as well as ideas that can be modified to meet a particular need. Many of the items may be used for noncommercial purposes by just including appropriate citations. You can read more about this resource at http://www.apa.org/pubs/databases/psyctests/.

Summary

We can use a one-time survey to understand something about a group of people at a point in time. This is sometimes called a *cross-sectional research design.*

We can use a survey to collect information about six dimensions of human functioning referred to as *the SCOPES model*: Social context, Cognition, Observable behavior patterns, Physiology, Emotion, and Spirituality.

There are several reasons why we should be careful in drawing conclusions about people from a one-time survey.

Concepts

Attitude	Field Theory
Belief	Hawthorne effect
Big Five	Knowledge

Cognition

Cross-sectional design

Demographics

Descriptive research

Lifespace

Opinion

SCOPES model

8. Assessing Social Context

Objectives:

> Identify demographic items relevant to respondents' social context.
>
> Identify the importance of relationships to social context.

It is common to ask identification questions that are linked to our social status. I often complete surveys asking for my age, sex or gender, education level, income, relationship status, employment status, family situation (e.g., how many children at home), ethnicity, religious affiliation, geographic location, and so forth. I will give some examples of ways these questions can be asked and comment on some of the difficulties.

People may not want to provide answers to some of these items for various reasons, including privacy concerns or feeling that the options do not apply. You may want to add options like *prefer not to answer* and *other* to confirm that the respondent considered your question but declined to answer it.

A source of questions about many items in this chapter is the U.S. Census Bureau. Their surveys often use terms in common use rather than terms preferred by social scientists. See https://www.census.gov for examples.

Basic Information

Age

Age is a continuous variable when you obtain a number in years. Depending on your sample, you can obtain a wide range of ages. Some programs will calculate age when you request a birthdate. You can also obtain age in years by providing a clickable list of ages to select or a blank for people to enter their age in years.

You can also obtain age by using categories. This has the advantage of protecting anonymity in small samples, but the statistical properties of categorical data limit statistical options. If you collect age as a continuous variable, you always have the option of grouping people by age categories when analyzing the data. Common age groups for adults include the following:

18-29
30-49
50-64
65 and older.

Consider the culture of your respondents when limiting responses to age groups. For example, senior citizens may live to more than 100 years. A 70-year-old might not share views similar to her 92-year-old father's.

Sex and Gender

There are problems in asking questions about sex and gender in many cultures because many people do not feel the traditional binary designations of sex (male/female) or gender (woman/man/ girl/boy) apply to them. *Sex* refers to biological status, and *gender* refers to a cultural status.

Consider why you think it important to include sex or gender in your survey. Also consider how the terms you use might offend some of the people who begin your survey and respond differently because they are offended by one or more terms used in the survey. On the one hand, people who do not identify with traditional terms for sex or gender may be offended when there are limited options. On the other hand, people who strongly identify as male or female, man or woman, might be offended by the variations in terms common in western cultures.

For those who believe they need to ask for sexual identity, consider adding *intersex, prefer not to say*, and *other* to the terms male and female. People with intersex conditions are born with variations in sex characteristics that do not meet typical definitions of male or female. Sex is an example of an item where the *prefer not to answer* or *other* options may be appropriate.

Variations in gender language can include more than two dozen terms. Examples of gender identity labels include *girl, boy, woman, man, transman, transwoman, bigender, pangender, prefer not to say,* and *other*. There are many other terms, and some lists mix the labels of sex identity (*male, female, intersex*) with the terms for gender. Research teams need to consider the culture of their respondents and the importance of collecting sex and gender information before adding sex or gender items to their surveys.

Education

Education levels vary with the culture. If education is important to your survey, consider the following categories:

- some high school
- high school diploma or equivalent,
- some college/technical/trade school,
- technical/trade school graduate,
- college graduate,
- master's degree,
- doctoral/ professional degree
- other

The *other* option allows people to report unique educational histories.

Ethnicity and Race

People often use the terms *race* and *ethnicity* interchangeably. The terms have varied over the years, so if race or ethnicity is important to your survey, then consider the culture of your respondents and use appropriate terms. For example, the United States has immigrants from many cultures from all over the world in addition to people associated with many Native American tribes. Many people report a mixed racial or ethnic heritage and may prefer checking more than one option. Again, *prefer not to answer* and *other* options can be helpful. Consider consulting the government surveys for the country and culture in which your survey will be administered.

The U.S. Census Bureau recognizes the difficulty with the terms *race* and *ethnicity*. If you are conducting a survey in the United States, you may wish to use the Census Bureau wording, which is closer to the way people think about race than the way professionals define the term. The Census Bureau defines each category and allows for identifying more than one category as well as writing in an identity. At publication, their categories are:

- American Indian or Alaska Native
- Asian
- Black or African American
- Native Hawaiian or Other Pacific Islander
- White

Census Link: https://www.census.gov/topics/population/race/about.html

Occupation and Employment

Some researchers are interested in employment status, such as part-time or full-time. In such cases it is best to be precise about number of hours worked in a typical week along with categories for those not employed. Sample options include the following:

- employed 40 or more hours per week
- employed 20-39 hours per week
- employed less than 20 hours per week
- not employed and looking for work
- not employed and not looking for work
- retired
- prefer not to answer
- other

If it is relevant to your survey goals, you may want to provide a list of occupational groups along with an *other* category. The list can be short or long depending on what is likely for your sample. Following are sample categories you could include:

- Legal
- Medical and health care
- Office and administrative support
- Business and finance
- Arts and entertainment
- Food services
- Education
- Social and community services

- Transportation
- Farming, fishing, forestry
- Other government services
- Architecture and engineering
- Sales
- Religious

If you are targeting a specific industry, you could clearly focus in on specific professions. For example, my colleagues and I have studied licensed or certified psychotherapists. Our list included counselors, social workers, pastoral counselors, chaplains, psychologists, psychiatrists, family therapists, and others.

Income

Income can be related to identity and the degree to which people access the resources in a society. Income can be a sensitive item, so it is usually good to consider adding both *prefer not to answer* and *other* response options. Some annual income categories that may be applicable to a wide sample in the United States may be the following:

under $10,000
$10,001 to $25,000
$25,001 to $40,000
$40,001 to $55,000
$55,001 to $75,000
$75,001 to $100,000
$100,001 to $150,000
$150,001 to $200,000
$200,001 and above

The examples are only suggestions, which should be adjusted to be appropriate for the culture. For example, some values are too low or too high for some samples within the United States. Obviously, outside the United States, other currencies and earning levels must be considered.

Relationships

Relationships can be described in many ways. We can consider family relationships, friendships, and romantic relationships.

Family relationships have been measured in many different ways. Rachel Pritchett and her colleagues found hundreds of measures, which they organized into six categories of quick and simple measures with a history of adequate reliability and validity data (Pritchett et al., 2011). Their six categories are parent-child relationships, parental practices and discipline, parental beliefs, marital quality, global family functioning, and situation specific. Given the number of measures in each category, I recommend obtaining the article and selecting measures best suited to your project.

Friend relationships measures address such factors as relationship quality, closeness, and function. The *McGill Friendship Questionnaire-Friendship Function* is a 30-item assessment of friendship quality designed for older adolescents and adults (Mendelson & Aboud, 1999). The measure has six subscales: stimulating companionship, help, intimacy, reliable alliance, self-validation, and emotional security. The items are rated on a 9-point scale from *never* (0) to *always* (8).

Friendship Ratings is a 12-item questionnaire rated on a 7-point scale from *not at all* (1) to *extremely* (7). A sample item is "My friend is responsive to my needs." This scale was used in a study by Denise Marigold and others (2014).

In social psychology, relationships are often examined in terms of degree of attachment. A scale that measures this characteristic is the *Adolescent Friendship Attachment Scale* (AFAS). The AFAS is a 30-item measure with three subscales: Secure, Anxious/Ambivalent, and Avoidant (Wilkinson, 2008).

Romantic relationships are often described in the following terms: *in a relationship, single, engaged, married, separated, divorced, remarried, prefer not to answer,* and *other.* We can also ask about the length of a relationship by requesting specific numbers of years or by asking respondents to check a list of years grouped by categories like 1-2 years, 3-5 years, and so forth.

Romantic relationships can also be assessed for quality, which has been assessed by measures of *satisfaction, adjustment,* and *happiness* (Graham et al., 2011). For example, Walter Schumm and his colleagues (1986) created the *Kansas Marital Satisfaction Scale,* which consists of three items rated on a 7-point scale ranging from *extremely dissatisfied* (1) to *extremely satisfied* (7). One of my students, Kelly McLeland, used the scale with both married and unmarried couples (McLeland & Sutton, 2005). It is common for researchers to modify items designed for married couples for use with unmarried couples (Graham et al., 2011).

The *Locke-Wallace Marital Adjustment Test* consists of 15 items scored in different ways (Locke & Wallace, 1959). In addition to an item about happiness, six items address feelings and thoughts toward a spouse, and eight items deal with relationship issues.

The *Couples Satisfaction Index* (Funk & Rogge, 2007) is a 32-item questionnaire that uses items from various other scales. One item asks for a ranking relationship satisfaction on a 7-point scale: "Please indicate the degree of happiness, all things considered, of your relationship." The other items use 6-point rating scales with variations in wording.

Religious Affiliation
I cover this topic in more depth in the "Assessing Spirituality" chapter. A problem with asking about religious affiliation is the incredible diversity of religious and spiritual groups with variations in beliefs, practices, and experiences.

Summary

Surveys commonly include demographic items important to identifying basic components of respondents' social contexts.

Some social items require careful thought and planning, such as wording questions about sex and gender or relationships.

Concepts
Census
Ethnicity, race
Gender
Intersex
Sex

9. Assessing Cognition

Objectives:

Identify ways to assess different types of thinking such as opinions, beliefs, and attitudes.

Identify three aspects of knowledge.

Cognition includes many subdomains such as memory, intelligence, thoughts, beliefs, and opinions. Qualified professionals can obtain sophisticated tests of memory, intelligence, and achievement from publishers. Most of these tests are expensive and require graduate training in tests and measurements to administer and interpret correctly. They may only be considered surveys in a very broad sense—as instruments that survey various aspects of memory, what people have learned, or how well they can solve standardized problems.

Surveys that assess thoughts, beliefs, and opinions are by nature diverse. Many surveys deal with what people think, so I will expand this cognition subsection to include subcategories and a few examples tied to a project to collect different types of thoughts related to a proposed sex-education program.

Opinions

Opinions represent judgments about a particular event or activity. Think of items that answer the question, "What do people think about ___?" The following statements could be presented as items to be rated from *strongly agree* to *strongly disagree*:

- Churches should provide sex education.

- Sex education should respect the religious traditions of all students.
- All public schools should include sex education at all grade levels.

Beliefs

Beliefs are important thoughts people hold as true about something. Beliefs are stronger than opinions and less likely to change than are opinions. Think of items that answer the question, "What do people believe about ___?" The following statements could be presented as items to be rated from *strongly agree* to *strongly disagree*:

- Condom use is an important component of sex education for teens.
- Sex education must be focused on abstinence until marriage.
- Information about safe sex has no place in sex education for teens.
- Sex educators ought to respect the teachings of major religious groups that believe premarital sex is sinful.

Attitudes: Focus on Cognition

Attitudes involve strong beliefs and feelings about acting in a specific way toward an event or activity. An attitude is a predisposition to act. In this section, I focus on the cognition (i.e., belief) aspect of an attitude. Think of items that answer the question, "What is their attitude toward ___?" We want to detect a tendency to act based on some combination of strong beliefs and feelings. Notice the phrasing "I would..." The following statements could be presented as items to be rated from *strongly agree* to *strongly disagree*:

- I would send my children to a sex-education program provided by my church.
- I would send my children to a sex-education program provided by my child's school.
- I would protest if a school teaches sex education that is contrary to my religious beliefs and values.

Knowledge

Knowledge consists of facts, concepts, and principles that are generally held to be true by experts in a particular field. Clearly, people can dispute facts, define concepts in various ways, and argue about the validity of certain principles. Think of items that answer the question, "What do people know about ___?" We could be more precise and ask what facts, concepts, or principles people know.

Following are some examples of items to ascertain knowledge related to sex education:

- What are the most effective methods of birth control? (facts)
- How do physicians determine fetal age? (fact)
- Define abortion. (concept)
- What factors predict the likelihood that a spouse will have an affair? (principle)

Summary

Cognition has to do with thoughts and images and includes processes of memory and problem-solving.

Special training is needed to use standardized tests of intelligence and other neuropsychological processes.

Surveys examine aspects of cognition when they ask for opinions, beliefs, and attitudes.

Cognition also includes knowledge, which may be assessed by asking about facts, concepts, and principles.

Concepts

Measures of
Attitudes
Beliefs
Knowledge
Opinion

10. Assessing Behavior Patterns
and Personality

Objectives:

Describe five broad personality traits evaluated with a variety of survey questions.

Identify items to assess leadership style.

Identify items to assess behavior patterns associated with values and strengths.

Personality traits have been researched for more than 100 years. A personality trait is a pattern of behavior that observers recognize as present for several years and in more than one social setting. Many survey questions are widely available to examine traits using a few items per trait. The fact that there are many traits that could be examined means the inclusion of personality items in a survey should be based on careful consideration of how important personality items are to the project.

The Big Five

Some researchers rely on freely available items to measure the Big Five personality traits mentioned previously. There are many versions of scales that measure the Big Five traits. In this section, I will provide an example of one item for each trait and provide the link to an online resource where you will find many items, including subscales for each trait. In one version, respondents are given the same stem for each item followed by a list of words that relate to one of the traits. The respondent does not see the category label, which I included in parentheses for your reference. Each item can be rated on a multipoint scale, such as *strongly agree* to *strongly disagree*. Note that the trait traditionally called *neuroticism* is often referred to by the positive dimension of *emotional stability*.

The stem reads, "I see myself as:"

- open to new experiences, complex (Openness)
- dependable, self-disciplined (Conscientiousness)
- extraverted, enthusiastic (Extraversion)
- sympathetic, warm (Agreeableness)
- anxious, easily upset (Neuroticism or Emotional Stability)

Research by Samuel Gosling and his colleagues (2002) revealed interesting contrasts between Big Five personality traits surveys completed based on friends' knowledge of a person and surveys completed by strangers—people who did not know the specific person but examined the place where they lived. In one study, the researchers administered a survey of the Big Five traits to university volunteers and a friend. Other respondents (strangers) rated the Big Five traits based on what they saw when entering the rooms where the volunteers lived. You might wonder what people would assume about your personality by your living space. Here's an example. Environmental cues suggesting *conscientiousness* were rooms that were well-organized, neat, and uncluttered.

It turns out that strangers who only saw the personal environments had the more accurate ratings for personality traits of Openness, Conscientiousness, and Emotional Stability. Friends were more accurate for ratings of Extraversion and Emotional Stability. In case you are wondering about the spelling of extraversion, psychological scientists retain the original spelling with an "a," but extroversion with an "o" is more common in the United States.

Leadership Traits

We are not limited to the Big Five. A number of other traits or behavior patterns may be highly relevant depending on the goals of your project. For example, leadership styles are recognizable behavior patterns. Following are some additional items measuring aspects of leadership.

Authentic Leadership Inventory (ALI)

The ALI measures authentic leadership based on four dimensions: Self-Awareness, Relational Transparency, Internalized Moral Perspective, and Balanced Processing (Neider & Schriesheim, 2011). Respondents complete this 14-item survey about a leader using a 5-point scale from *Disagree strongly* (1) to *Agree strongly* (5).

Charismatic Leadership Scale

Charismatic leaders are known for their ability to motivate people. Respondents complete the 8-item Charismatic Leadership Scale developed by De Hoogh and colleagues (2005) to rate a leader on a 7-point scale from *strongly disagree* (1) to *strongly agree* (7). A sample item is "Emphasizes the importance of being committed to our values and beliefs."

Multifactor Leadership Questionnaire—Form 1

This lengthy survey consists of 73 items (Bycio et al., 1995). Using principal-components analysis, the researchers found three transformational leadership factors: Charismatic, Individualized Consideration, and Intellectual Stimulation. Two transactional factors were also present: Contingent Reward and Management-by-Exception. Each of the items is rated on a 5-point scale from *not at all* (0) to *frequently* (4). A sample Intellectual Stimulation item is "Gives personal attention to members who seem neglected." A sample Management-by-Exception item is, "Only tells me what I have to know to do my job."

Values and Strengths

Character strengths may be considered an aspect of personality. A measure available online is the *Values in Action* survey commonly known by the acronym *VIA*. As of this writing, the VIA was freely available at www.viacharacter.org. The adult VIA is available in 39 translations, and the youth version in 18 translations. In 2017, the site reported use of the VIA in 196 countries. The VIA measures 24 strengths in six categories. Following are the six categories with the subscales:

- Wisdom [Creativity, Curiosity, Judgment, Love of Learning, Perspective]
- Courage [Bravery, Honesty, Perseverance, Zest]
- Humanity [Kindness, Love, Social Intelligence]
- Justice [Fairness, Leadership, Teamwork]
- Temperance [Forgiveness, Humility, Prudence, Self-regulation]
- Transcendence [Appreciation of Beauty, Gratitude, Hope, Humor, Spirituality]

The VIA has been used in hundreds of studies. An example of use in the workplace involved 686 participants. Littman-Ovadia and Lavy (2015) found that the character strength perseverance had the highest correlation with work productivity and the lowest correlation with counter-productive behavior. The authors opined that meaningfulness and views of work as a career and calling explained the relationships.

Summary

In the SCOPES model, observable behavior patterns are personality traits, which are present for years and across situations.

Researchers who consider personality relevant to their project often include items that measure one or more of the Big Five personality traits.

An example of a specific aspect of behavior affecting the lives of most people is leadership. Surveys have been developed to assess leadership style.

Values and strengths are additional aspects of personality that have been studied extensively. One popular measure is the VIA.

Concepts

Measurement of
> Big Five personality traits
> Leadership traits or styles
> Values and strengths

11. Assessing Physical Health

Objectives:

Identify examples of survey items associated with physiology.

Identify likely connections between a person's physiological status and other aspects of functioning.

Suppose after seeing so many photos of exciting trips online, you decide to take the plunge—perhaps a cruise. Chances are you will complete a health questionnaire. It's no fun to be on the trip of a lifetime and unable to enjoy it due to a medical event. Soon after my son married, I was excited about taking them home to meet my family in London. I selected a UK tour but had some pretty bad pain on a bus in Edinburgh. It turned out to be my first kidney stone attack. Fortunately, I was only out of action for one day. And my family didn't mind missing part of the trip to be with me. Governments and tour companies often require us to complete medical or health question-naires—surveys. You may have to respond to statements with a simple *yes* or *no*. If you need a health questionnaire because you are leading a trip, check with your organization, tour group company, and government website. Laws and regulations vary. Keep in mind that health questions can be intrusive, so follow applicable ethical guidelines and policies.

Following are a few examples of health questionnaire items I have encountered.

Name as it appears on passport _____

Address _____

City _____

Country _____

Zip/Post code _____

Contact phone _____

Email _____

Do you have any special dietary needs?

What food or medication allergies do you have?

What is your physical fitness level?

Have you been hospitalized recently? When and why?

Do you have any heart-related conditions?

What medications are you taking?

What additional information may be useful to emergency medical personnel in the event of an emergency?

You can imagine that questions about health and illness could require an entire book full of items related to medical conditions. Once again, we will need to limit ourselves to items that are relevant to the purpose of our project. For example, we may want to ask simple items to identify if a person is under the care of a health care professional or takes medication that interferes with some aspect of life. We may need to know how many people require special accommodations to experience an educational program or access a building.

If you have been to a health care provider lately, chances are you completed a form that asks questions about your general health, mental health, medications, and other facts that can help providers screen for more serious concerns in addition to any symptoms of concern. Because health is an area of specialization with so many categories, it is best to consult with a local licensed or certified health provider for items relevant to specific survey projects. An example of health screening categories can be found at MedlinePlus: https://medlineplus.gov/healthscreening.html.

Examples of Health Surveys

My purpose in this short section is to offer some examples of brief surveys that address health concerns affecting large numbers of people around the world. Various government and private organizations provide questionnaires to identify serious conditions. Information about prevention and treatment can be found on their websites.

The abuse of substances like alcohol and other drugs is a worldwide concern. Substance abuse has wide-ranging health effects not only on the user but also on family, friends, neighbors, employers, and community organizations. Many screening surveys exist to help individuals, community service personnel, and families identify possible problems that should be investigated with more detailed surveys and interviews. A short screening resource is the three-item AUDIT-C designed to screen for alcohol use disorders. Each item asks patients to respond to a question with one of five response options. A sample item is "How many standard drinks containing alcohol do you have on a typical day?" The answers range from 1-2 to 10 or more. Other resources are available at https://www.integration.samhsa.gov/clinical-practice/screening-tools#drugs.

Dementia is a rapidly growing concern as about 47 million people had the condition in 2015 and a threefold increase is expected by 2050 (Livingston et al., 2017). What these numbers don't tell is the additional impact on family and friends involved in providing or organizing care. Family members can struggle with demands on time, energy, finances, and managing emotions. Several screening tools are available. A short survey designed to help primary care providers collect information from family members is the *Family Questionnaire* available from the Alzheimer's Association (alz.org). Five items are rated on a 4-point scale from *not at all* to *does not apply*. A sample item is "repeating or asking the same thing over and over."

The National Stroke Association (stroke.org) has important information presented in a creative way. The four-item survey uses the acronym *FAST* and encourages people to call the U.S. emergency number 911 if any signs are present. Getting to a hospital quickly improves the odds of a better recovery. The response rating is straightforward—a sign is either present or absent.

F = **FACE**: Ask the person to smile. Does one side of the face droop?
A = **ARMS**: Ask the person to raise both arms. Does one arm drift downward?
S = **SPEECH**: Ask the person to repeat a simple phrase. Is their speech slurred or strange?
T = **TIME**: If you observe any of these signs, call 911 immediately.

An example of a health-related survey that may be useful in a community setting has to do with literacy. The *Brief Health Literacy Screen* has five items rated on a 5-point scale, which changes with the item (Sand-Jecklin & Coyle, 2014). A sample item is "How often do you have problems learning about your health because of trouble understanding written health information?" To give you an example of the breadth of surveys available, I found 77 entries just for the key words *health literacy* in the PsycTESTS database.

Health and Faith

Many religious people pray for healing when they are ill. Recently, researchers have become increasingly aware of the importance of spirituality in health care settings. One example of a five-item survey that addresses this integration is the Healing Index (Sutton et al., 2014). Each of five items is rated on a 5-point scale from *strongly disagree* (1) to *strongly agree* (5). An example item is "I have prayed for the sick and they've been healed."

Forgiveness is a virtue in many religions. Researchers have documented links between forgiveness and physiological indicators of lowered stress, including the stress hormone, *cortisol*, muscle tension, heart rate, and blood pressure. (For a review of forgiveness and health, see Worthington et al., 2007.) For an example of forgiveness survey items, see the "Assessing Spirituality" chapter.

Summary

Understanding people includes understanding their physiological condition or health. Although health conditions may not be a part of a survey project, it is important to remember that all people have bodies in various states of health, which affects other aspects of functioning.

Health care professionals use screening tools, which are short surveys to identify signs and symptoms that may indicate more serious conditions.

Some surveys that ask a few questions and guide people in finding help are available online.

As with all surveys, those creating or using surveys of health conditions must follow ethical guidelines. Consultation with a licensed or certified health provider is important before addressing health concerns in a survey.

12. Assessing Emotions and Attitudes

Objectives:

Identify examples of surveys that address common emotional states.

Identify examples of surveys that assess attitudes.

As noted previously, scientists disagree on which emotions are the core emotions, but there are some measures than can be helpful. Psychologists have used the term *affect* to refer to the present experience of emotion or feeling. Affect is often contrasted with *mood,* which refers to an emotional state over a longer period of time, such as feeling happy or sad or angry most days.

I included a section on attitudes because attitudes are a combination of emotions and cognitions that often lead to action. As previously noted, attitudes are predispositions. In this section, I focus on attitudes that have an emotional focus in addition to the cognitive element of belief. Many surveys are designed to measure attitudes. I have included a few examples of those that seem to emphasize feeling over cognition.

Emotions, Feelings, and Affect

Positive and Negative Affect Schedule (PANAS)

A questionnaire widely used in research is known by its acronym *PANAS*, that is, the *Positive and Negative Affect Schedule* (Watson et al., 1988). There are 10 items to measure positive and negative affect. Examples of positive affect include enthusiastic, alert, and excited. Examples of negative affect include ashamed, guilty, and afraid.

Anger Scales

I include the *Anger Scales* because they offer a look at a collection of 37 items that assess anger in detail—including a look at antecedents to anger and ways anger is expressed. The items are rated from *not at all typical* (1) to *very typical* (4). The scale was developed by Alonso-Arbiol and colleagues (2011).

Fear Inventory III

Fear is a common emotion, and most agree it is a core feeling. Fear surveys are available for children and adults. Many of the fear surveys assess a fear of something such as animals, food, or pain. I selected the *Fear Inventory III* (Taylor & Rachman, 1992) as an example because it includes 66 items organized in seven subscales: Social Anxiety, Agoraphobic Fears, Fear of Bodily Injury, Death and Illness, Fear of Exposure to Sex/Aggressive Stimuli, Fear of Harmless Animals, Fear of Sadness, and Fear of Anxiety. The items are rated on a 5-point scale from *not at all* (0) to *very much* (4).

Subjective Happiness Scale

Happiness may be the quintessential positive feeling state. We commonly wish others a happy birthday or anniversary. The *Subjective Happiness Scale* is a short four-item survey developed by Sonja Lyubomirsky and Heidi Lepper (1999) and has been completed by thousands of respondents. The items are rated on 7-point scales that use different words to describe the end points. A sample item calls for ratings of *less happy* (1) to *more happy* (7): "Compared to most of my peers, I consider myself…"

Attitudes: Focus on Emotion/Motivation

Gratitude Questionnaire

Gratitude is a valuable attitude linked to many positive experiences and feeling grateful. This short six-item survey assesses a person's predisposition to experience gratitude (McCullough et al., 2002). The items are rated *strongly disagree* (1) to *strongly agree* (7). A sample item is "I have so much in life to be thankful for."

Adult Hope Scale

This 12-item measure of hope is based on C. R. Snyder's hope theory, which posits that hope is a motivational state composed of agency and pathways (Snyder et al., 1991). *Agency* consists of energy focused on achieving a goal, and *pathways* are plans to reach a goal. Agency and pathways are subtests measured by four items. The scale also contains four filler items, which are not always included by other researchers. A few of us used Snyder's scale in research and found hope is positively correlated with both compassion and forgiveness (Sutton et al., 2014).

Faith-Based Policy Attitude Scales

There are 15 items organized into four subscales to assess attitudes toward faith-based policies (Choma et al., 2016). I included these scales as examples of how to write items to address attitudes toward policies in general and faith-based policies in particular. Although specific items and their wording (they reference Canada) may not work as written, concerns about policies and related social issues can be addressed by items using similar wording. The items are rated on a 7-point scale from *strongly disagree* (1) to *strongly agree* (7). An example of faith-based schooling is "I am in support of publicly funded Catholic schools." An example of an item about religious symbols in schools is "Only small (discreet) religious symbols should be allowed in Canadian schools or government offices."

Summary

Understanding people requires understanding their emotions. Emotions play a role in motivation and are closely linked to thoughts.

Several surveys address common emotions, such as happiness, fear, and anger.

Emotions are often linked to beliefs in forming an attitude. I provided examples of gratitude and hope measures as well as an attitude toward policies survey.

13. Assessing Spirituality

Objective:

Identify examples of survey items that address spirituality.

I will refer to several examples of questions assessing spirituality. Many of the items are grouped together to form a short scale with a unifying theme. Some of the scales may be used without permission, but you would need to cite the source in reports and presentations. You will find more information in the appendices, including specific items that may be used in your survey projects.

Brief Multidimensional Measure of Religiousness/Spirituality (BMMRS)

This measure is available from fetzer.org. It contains 38 items organized in several groups or subscales. Statistical properties are available in a downloadable report booklet. At the time of this writing, there was no charge to use the items. I will describe a few of the subscales to show the range of items available. The subscales are in italics.

Daily Spiritual Experiences is a six-item measure. Each item is rated on a scale from *many times a day* (1) to *never or almost never* (6). A sample item is "I feel God's presence."

Private Religious Practices is a four-item measure. Each item is rated on a 6-point scale from *more than once a day* (1) to *once a month* (6). A sample item is "How often do you pray privately in places other than at church?"

Religious and Spiritual Coping is a seven-item measure. Items are rated on a 4-point scale from *a great deal* (1) to *not at all* (4). A sample item is "I think about how my life is part of a larger spiritual force."

Religious Support is a four-item measure to find out how much support congregants expect to receive from their congregations. The items are rated on a 4-point scale from *a great deal* (1) to *none* (4). A sample item is "If you were ill, how much would the people in your congregation help you out?"

Religious commitment is an important aspect of faith measured on a brief scale, which includes a mix of five items measured in different ways. One example rated on a 6-point scale—*more than once a week* (1) to *never* (6)—is "How often do you go to religious services?" An open-ended item asks the average amount of contributions per month or year.

Santa Clara Strength of Religious Faith Questionnaire
This 10-item measure developed by Plante and Boccaccini (1997) asks respondents to rate each item from *strongly disagree* (1) to *strongly agree* (4). A sample item is "My religious faith is extremely important to me." A five-item version is also available (Plante et al., 2002).

Duke University Religious Index (DUREL)
This scale has five items about religious beliefs or involvement (Koenig et al., 1997). A sample item is "How often do you spend time in private religious activities such as prayer, meditation, or Bible study?"

Religious Commitment Inventory—10 (RCI—10)

The RCI—10, developed by Everett L. Worthington, Jr. and his colleagues, uses 10 items rated on a 5-point scale to measure religious commitment (Worthington et al., 2003). Each item is rated from *not at all true of me* (1) to *totally true of me* (5). A sample item is "I often read books and magazines about my faith."

Brief RCOPE

The *Brief RCOPE* uses 14 items to measure how people rely on their faith to cope with negative events (Pargament et al., 2000). The items address positive and negative coping by asking respondents to rate the items from *not at all* (1) to *a great deal* (4). A sample item is "Looked for a stronger connection with God."

Intratextual Fundamentalism Scale (IFS)

The *Intratextual Fundamentalism Scale* (Williamson et al., 2010) measures the extent to which religious people rely on their sacred texts. The items are rated using a 6-point response format from *strongly disagree* (1) to *strongly agree* (5). A sample item is "Everything in the Sacred Text is absolutely true."

Chapter Note

I have included examples of spirituality items in appendix F, which you may use in teaching and research by simply citing the reference. Additional permission is not required for non-commercial use.

Summary

Understanding people often requires understanding their spirituality, which may be defined in many ways.

Global perspectives on spirituality focus on meaning, but spirituality also includes specific beliefs, practices, and experiences.

Some surveys attempt to measure aspects of spirituality that are part of many religious traditions, such as prayer.

Some surveys are specific to religious traditions yet attempt to identify diversity, such as the range of beliefs, practices, and experiences found among Christians.

Part III:

Understanding Basic Designs and Statistics

14. Using Surveys to Evaluate Workshops

Objectives:

Identify ways to use surveys to evaluate workshops and similar educational programs.

Identify factors to consider when drawing conclusions from different research designs.

In this chapter, I will consider some ways surveys can help evaluate the effectiveness of a workshop or other educational program. In the previous chapters, we considered what type of survey we wanted to create. Thus, we considered evaluating opinions, beliefs, attitudes, and so forth. In this chapter, we focus on a few research designs that can be used to evaluate a workshop.

A research design is a plan for carrying out the research. Surveys may be as simple as two to five items or quite complex, including several subtopics. Likewise, plans to carry out a survey vary from simple to complex. Some plans are better than others. In the language of research, plans are called *research designs*. In a very simple design, a researcher administers a survey at the end of a workshop. Although administering surveys at the end of a workshop provides some information, it is not the best way to conduct research.

Basic Experimental Designs

The experiment is the gold standard of scientific research. The effectiveness of a workshop or other educational program can be studied using surveys within an experimental design. In an experiment, the research team controls the independent variable and measures the dependent variable. A workshop or similar educational program becomes a two-group independent variable when some people participate in the workshop and some people do not. In a true experiment, the research team randomly assigns people to either the workshop or the no-workshop group. At the conclusion of the workshop, the research team collects evidence of change using a survey. The survey measures the dependent variable.

A Two-Group Study

A research team wishes to study the effectiveness of a forgiveness education program. After reading about the REACH model developed by Everett L. Worthington Jr. (2006) at Virginia Commonwealth University, they decide to implement the program in a weekend format. The research team formulates a simple hypothesis: that the REACH forgiveness program will help people forgive someone.

In this example, forgiveness is the independent variable having two levels or groups formed by randomly assigning participants to the REACH workshop or the control group. The control group does not attend the REACH workshop. At the conclusion of the workshop, all the people in the study complete a forgiveness survey, which asks questions to determine how forgiving they are toward a person who offended them. The forgiveness survey measures the dependent variable, which is forgiveness. Notice that forgiveness is used in two ways. Forgiveness is both the independent and dependent variable. As an independent variable, forgiveness is defined as participation or nonparticipation in the REACH forgiveness workshop. As a dependent variable, forgiveness is a state of forgiveness measured by a score on a forgiveness survey.

After the surveys have been completed, the data are analyzed. A common statistical analysis to analyze data from a two-group study is the *t* test, which will be discussed in more detail later. The test results will indicate the REACH workshop was effective if people who took the workshop produced higher scores than did people in the no-workshop control group.

The research team will draw a conclusion about the effectiveness of the REACH model based on the results. If they have maintained adequate control over the research process and found significantly different forgiveness scores for those who participated in the workshop, they may conclude that the workshop caused the change. When statistics are used to infer something about a population based on the results of a study, they are called *inferential statistics*. In this case, the research team wishes to draw a conclusion about the effectiveness of the REACH model they hope will be true if they were to use the program in the future.

A key to drawing conclusions is maintaining adequate control. The research team will have to ensure that the workshop was delivered as intended if they are to draw valid conclusions about the REACH model. Researchers exercise control in various ways, such as by providing workshop leaders with a manual that guides them through activities for each component of a workshop. In addition, leaders should have the opportunity to practice the delivery of the workshop with feedback from the research team.

Researchers also need to be concerned about the activities of people in the control group. If some of the control group members are interested in forgiveness and read a self-help forgiveness book, then they might have higher forgiveness scores than would otherwise be the case if they did something else. It is often best to have control group participants engage in some neutral activity during a study. Researchers should at least ask questions to determine if control group members were involved in any activities that might affect forgiveness scores.

During a study, researchers monitor the delivery of the workshop to ensure it was delivered as planned. Any deviations from the workshop manual may make the workshop so unique that they could not conclude that the outcomes would apply to future workshops.

Finally, the items mentioned in the section about drawing conclusions following a descriptive study apply here as well. People change in response to personal and external events. People leave workshops and control groups for various reasons. People respond to being in a study. And a combination of events can affect the outcomes of any study. These uncontrolled events are referred to as *extraneous variables*. If the extraneous variables are known to influence the scores on the survey, they are called *confounding variables*.

The Research Process

In this section, I will summarize the steps of the research process illustrated in the previous section. The steps apply to both simple and complex experiments, but my summary will focus on a workshop experiment. I will use the term *workshop* as a generic term for any educational program such as a seminar, group experience, or even a college course.

1. Review previous research on a topic of interest. Pay attention to studies of effective and ineffective workshops, seminars, and educational programs.
2. Formulate a hypothesis indicating what you expect to change as a result of participating in the workshop.

3. Obtain a sample of participants and randomly assign them to either the workshop group or the no-workshop control group.

4. Establish controls. Ensure the workshop is delivered in a standardized way by providing a leader's guide (workshop manual) and observing to ensure the leader stays on track. Decide what the control group should do to ensure other experiences do not interfere with understanding the results.

5. Select survey items to measure the desired outcome or outcomes. For example, are you measuring changes in opinions, beliefs, attitudes, knowledge, behavior, or satisfaction?

6. Use a survey to collect the results.

7. Analyze the results using appropriate statistical tests.

8. Interpret the results in view of how well the team was able to control extraneous variables that could influence the final score.

9. Present the results.

A Multi-Group Study

Research designs can quickly become more complex. If you are going to all the trouble to conduct a study, sometimes it doesn't take much effort to add a little complexity to make the effort more worthwhile. For example, suppose we added a third group to the forgiveness study. In addition to the two groups—the REACH workshop group and the control group—we could add a group that reads a self-help book on forgiveness. It so happens that Worthington has published a book about forgiveness (2003). I probably should make a disclosure here. Everett L. Worthington Jr. is a friend, but I do not get any income from the sale of his books.

The analysis of the data also becomes more complex. A common procedure is to use an ANOVA, which helps researchers detect overall differences when there are two or more groups. If the overall results are significant, the researchers will need to find out how each group fared. For example, did one group have much higher forgiveness scores than the other two groups? Did the workshop group and the self-help group do better than the control group while the workshop group was still the most effective method? As before, the research team will need to determine if there were any factors that could influence forgiveness scores outside of the workshop and self-help group activities.

A Nonexperimental Workshop Design:

Pretest and Posttest Surveys

Pretest surveys offer researchers the advantage of seeing how people change before and after a workshop. But we will still need a control group to ensure that any identified changes were likely due to the workshop and not just the passage of time or score variations in taking a survey twice.

There are some problems in giving a pretest. The questions in a pretest survey introduce information to people who take the survey. Those questions provide some guidance as to the content of the workshop. If people remember the pretest items, then their performance on the posttest can be influenced by the pretest. Pretests may also build hope when the questions cause respondents to think about the things they will learn. We cannot assume that changes evident on a posttest survey are due to the educational experience. Both the pretest and the educational experience can influence posttest results.

For example, suppose an organization offers a marriage seminar. Before the seminar, researchers ask participants to complete a survey about their marriage. As they answer questions about commitment, communication, and other issues, they become aware of common topics in a marriage seminar. In addition, the pretest can induce hope that their marriage will improve as a result of the seminar. In similar situations, pretest surveys create expectancy effects, which in turn add to the seminar experience and can become evident on the posttest. Now you may consider this induction of hope to be a good thing. And surely, a program that helps people enjoy a better marriage is good. Nevertheless, we must wonder how much is due to the pretest effects versus the seminar itself. We cannot eliminate the pretest effects by using a control group, but we can at least compare how much each group changed from the pretest to the posttest by looking at the differences in the *change scores*. Change scores are the differences between scores on the posttest minus the scores on the pretest.

Summary

We can use surveys to evaluate the effectiveness of a workshop or other educational program.

The two-group design is a simple experimental design in which researchers randomly assign people to one of two groups of the independent variable, such as a workshop or no-workshop group, called the *control group*. At the end of the workshop, a survey is used to collect information relevant to the workshop goals.

Research designs can become more complex by adding additional groups.

Only controlled experiments allow researchers to draw conclusions about cause and effect relationships between the independent and dependent variables.

When random assignment is not possible or desirable, researchers can use a pretest to identify the status of the groups at the beginning of the study. At the end of the study, researchers can examine change scores for each of the groups.

In any study, there are extraneous variables beyond the control of the research team that must be considered when interpreting the results.

Concepts

Change scores   Inferential statistics
Confounding variable   Multi-group study
Control group   Pretest–posttest study
Dependent variable   Random assignment
Experiment   Research designs
Extraneous variable   Two-group study
Independent variable

15. Understanding Survey Results: Part 1

Objectives:

Identify four scales of measurement.

Define and give examples of frequency data and percentages.

Define three measures of central tendency: Mean, Median, Mode.

Many newspapers include charts displaying the results of a poll or survey along with a few numbers. In this chapter, I will review some of the basic statistics that summarize the results of a survey. In the next chapter, I will describe some common charts used to present the numbers in an easy to grasp format.

Understanding Numbers

Statisticians refer to four types of numbers. We need to know the type of number used in a survey in order to understand the results. In surveys, numbers are used to identify or measure something. Measurement systems are known as scales. In this section, I will present four measurement scales.

Nominal Scale

The nominal scale identifies categories. We can assign numbers to identify different groups of people or organizations. We can refer to groups with team names like *Tigers* or *Panthers*. When we use numbers in a nominal scale, the numbers just refer to the names of the categories and higher numbers do not mean more of an item or a particular order. Sometimes numbers are used to code something about people in a database. Following are some examples:

- People associated with a church could be identified in a database by a number for example: 1 = active church member, 2 = inactive church member, 3 = nonmember regularly attending church and so forth.
- Ethnic groups labeled using a number based on perceived continent of origin such as European or South American.
- Employment status can be identified by using numbers for Employed, Unemployed, Retired, and so forth.
- Residence can be coded by geographic region for example: 1 = Northeast, 2 = Southwest, and so forth.

Ordinal Scale

A second scale is the ordinal scale. The numbers in an ordinal scale reflect a rank order. The numbers mean that in some way, one rank is more than another rank. People rank themselves or others on a characteristic from high to low. The quantitative difference between the ranks one and two and the ranks two and three could be very different. The ordinal scale does not recognize the size of these differences between rankings. Ordinal scales only recognize the order of the rank.

Following are examples of rankings that could be in a survey:

- After listing your conference topic preferences, order the top five from most to least favorite.
- Considering the music this morning, on a scale from 1 to 10, how would you rate the quality if 10 is the best it has ever been?
- List your current courses and rank them from high to low based on your interest level.

- Look at these five workshop proposals and rank them from 1 to 5 where 5 represents your top-rated proposal.

Interval Scale

The third measurement scale is the interval scale. The difference between values on an interval scale are considered to be equal. Although scientists sometimes debate the merits of the equality of the intervals, that debate is beyond the scope of this book. Common examples of interval scales may include:

- A survey that measures conceptual knowledge following an instructional program or course.
- A survey that measures personality traits such as agreeableness and conscientiousness.
- A survey that measures relationship skills such as communication and conflict resolution.

Ratio Scale

Finally, the ratio scale is similar to the interval scale as far as equal intervals, but the ratio scale has a true zero point. Examples of ratio scales include tape measures to measure height or length and scales that measure weight. In the cases of height and weight, it is reasonable to refer to ratios. For example, a person weighing 250 pounds is twice as heavy as a person who weighs 125 pounds. An important point about ratio scales is that true ratios do not exist for the other three measurement scales. It does not make sense to say that a person is two times more agreeable or depressed than another person.

Following are some examples of ratio scales.

- An expansion proposal that doubles the number of cars that can be parked.

- A building proposal that increases the square footage for classrooms by 75%.
- A program expansion to serve 50% more students.
- An analysis of donations indicating an increase of 10% over last year's record.

Describing Samples

In this section, I will present some of the common ways statisticians report data they obtain from surveys. I will include the concepts of frequency, percentage, and central tendency.

Frequencies

Frequencies are the number of people who respond in a particular way. If 25 people identified as prolife then we would write $f = 25$ for the prolife response. In our hypothetical example, we might find that $f = 5$ reporting prochoice and $f = 5$ who either chose the option *no opinion* or did not provide an answer. Researchers use the letter n for the number of people and often use the letter X for a score. The letters are in italics. The f for frequency is lower case and the n is lower case for a sample or portion of a sample. Use an upper-case N for all of the people in a dataset or population.

Percentages

According to pewforum's landscape study, 70.6% of the U.S. identify as Christian. Most people have a general sense of what percentages mean and percentages are easier to explain than more advanced analyses. Consider reporting percentages when reporting the results of your survey. You can usually obtain percentages from spreadsheet programs.

Use the percent symbol (%) when reporting percentages. If you found that 35% of employees read their handbook in the past year you would know that for any representative sample of 100 people, 35 of them would have read their handbook last year. You calculate percentage by dividing the number of people who read their handbook by the number of people in your sample and multiplying the result by 100.

Consider another example. Suppose you wish to know how many students in a small college regularly eat breakfast defined as eating breakfast at least five mornings each week. First, you analyze data from last year and find that of 1,000 students, 200 eat breakfast. So far you know $N = 1000$ for the total number of students and $n = 200$ for the group who reported having breakfast. If you divide 200 by 1000 and multiple by 100 you find 20% eat breakfast ($200 \div 1000 \times 100 = 20\%$).

Percent means per hundred. One percent is one hundredth of a whole. A percentage is 100 times a proportion.

Understanding Averages and Central Values

Averages help us identify what is typical of a data set. Averages are shorthand ways of knowing something about people or an organization. Two common types of averages are mean and median. A more precise concept is *central tendency*, which refers to data that represent the center of a distribution of values or scores. In large data sets containing information about people, most data fall near the middle with smaller percentages falling above and below the middle values. Three common measures of central tendency are the mode, the median, and the mean.

Mode

The mode is the most frequent value in a data set. The symbol for the mode is *Mo*. Suppose five staff members earn the following scores on a leadership scale [20, 21, 22, 24, 21]. The most frequent score is 21 so the mode = 21. The modal value can vary more than the Median and the Mean so it is often ignored or only reported along with the Median or Mean, which are more stable. Stable values are those less likely to be different in another sample.

Median

The median is the middle value in a dataset. The symbol for the median is *Mdn*. As the middle value, the median is at the 50th percentile. The median divides a set of values in half so that half the values are above and below the median. To find the median, arrange a set of values in order from high to low then choose the middle number. For example, suppose seven students earn the following scores on a history questionnaire [41, 42, 40, 47, 41, 49, 44]. First, we place the scores in order from high to low as follows [49, 47, 44, 42, 41, 41, 40]. Next, we find the middle value, which would be the fourth value. Thus, the median = 42. There are three scores above and below the median.

Suppose eight faculty members are rated on various attributes and obtain the following total ratings [77, 81, 83, 83, 85, 86, 86, 86]. The median for this set is 84 but 84 does not appear in the data set. We use the number 84 because it is midway between the two middle values of 83 and 85. As you can see, four numbers are above and below the number 84. When there are an even number of values, the median is the average of the two middle values. You can simply add 83 + 85 to get 168 then divide 168 by 2 to get 84. When there are an odd number of values in a data set, the median is the middle value.

Mean
The mean is the arithmetic average of the values in a dataset. The symbol for the mean is *M*. To obtain the average you add all of the values and divide by the number of values. For example, five people on a committee take annual leave totaling the following number of days off [18, 21, 22, 23, 16]. When we add the five values, they total 100. If we divide 100 by the number of values (i.e., number of people), which is 5, we obtain a value of 20. The mean of the set of values is 20. Thus, on average, these committee members take 20 days of annual leave.

Let me illustrate this another way. First add the values: 18+21+22+23+16 = 100. Then divide the sum of the values (100) by the number of values (5) to find the average value of 20. Notice that none of the committee members took an annual leave of exactly 20 days. The number 20 represents an average number of days of annual leave taken by the people in the sample. Because the mean requires us to average every value in a dataset, it is more sensitive to the values in a dataset than either the mode or the median, which only consider the most frequent or the middle values.

When a set of values includes one or more values that are very different from most values, the mean is not the best value to report. In fact, reporting a mean can be misleading. Scores or values that are very different from most scores or values are called *outliers*. Outliers keep us from understanding what is typical of a dataset. For example, suppose we want to know the typical age of staff in a youth organization. We learn that the mean age is 36 but if most staff members are below age 30, the mean does not provide an accurate picture of our hypothetical data set, which includes the following ages [28, 29, 26, 27, 70]. In this case, the *Mdn* of 28 is a better measure of central tendency than the mean because the median is less affected by extreme scores. In most cases, it is more accurate to report median values for salaries and ages than mean values because very high or low numbers can change the value reported as average or typical.

Resources

You can find a lot of surveys at www.pewforum.org.
The religious landscape data mentioned in this chapter can be found at http://www.pewforum.org/religious-landscape-study/

Summary

There are four measurement scales: nominal, ordinal, interval, and ratio scales.

In survey research, a frequency is the number of times the same response occurs. A percentage refers to a fraction of a whole for example, half of the sample means 50% of the sample.

The mode, median, and mean are central values in a distribution of values or scores.

The median is more typical of the average value than the mean in some distributions like salaries and possibly ratings of teachers.

Concepts

Central tendency   Median
Frequencies   Mode
Interval scale   Ordinal scale
Nominal scale   Percentages
Mean   Ratio scale

16. Understanding Survey Results Part 2

Objectives:

Define range and standard deviation.

Identify the commonly referred to percentage of scores linked to the normal curve.

Describe the concept of correlation between sets of scores.

Describe how researchers look for significant differences between groups of data.

Range and Standard Deviation

In the previous chapter, I presented three measures of central tendency. Obviously, the mode, median, and mean only provide a limited idea about the values in a dataset. It is interesting to know an average score or value but we often want more. In this section, I will discuss ranges and standard deviations.

Range

The range is the difference between the highest and lowest value in a dataset. Suppose we have measured marital satisfaction for ten seminar participants who obtain the following scores [25, 22, 19, 20, 26, 23, 21, 20, 24, 20]. We find that $M = 22$ and $Mdn = 21.50$. In this case, the range = 7, that is, 26 – 19 = 7. The range provides a general idea of the spread of scores in a data set. However, suppose we change one score so that instead of 26, one person scored 30. Now $M = 22.4$ and $Mdn = 21.50$ (no change) but the range is 30 - 19 = 11 One score can make a major difference in the range thus we can say the range statistic is not very stable. Notice also that the mean was pulled upward by the higher score but the middle value or Median did not change. Some statistics programs and reports refer to the highest value as *Max* for maximum value and the lowest value as *Min* for minimum value. Thus, using the language of Max and Min, Range = Max – Min.

Standard Deviation

A more common statistic to describe a set of scores or data is the standard deviation symbolized by an upper case italicized *SD* when writing reports or creating tables. When data are normally distributed, the standard deviation provides information about how far a particular value or score is from the mean of the sample. The normal distribution is a bell-shaped curve often called the *normal curve.*

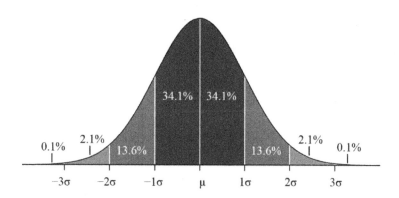

The numbers below the curve are in standard deviation units. The zero is set at the middle of the curve. In a normal distribution of data, the mean, median, and mode are at the mid-point of zero. The height of the curve represents the number of values or scores. As you can see, the curve is highest in the middle thus, most people score in the middle on many characteristics such as personality traits.   Technically,   the curve never touches the baseline leaving room for a small fraction of a percentage of data at the extreme ends. In statistics texts, the right and left ends of the curve are referred to as *tails*. And the points where there is a slight change in the curve at +/1 one standard deviation are referred to as *inflection points*.

The mathematical properties of the curve provide helpful guidelines for knowing more about a score or other value when we know the mean and standard deviation of a dataset.

Here are some percentages that will provide a general idea of where scores fall.

68% of scores fall between + 1 and – 1 Standard Deviations from the mean.

95% of scores fall between + 2 and – 2 Standard Deviations from the mean.

99% of scores fall between + 3 and – 3 Standard Deviations from the mean.

In the previous example of ten people taking a marital satisfaction survey, the mean was 22. I calculated the standard deviation to be 2.40. Based on these two pieces of information, we can say that 68% of our scores fall between 19.60 and 24.40. I obtained 19.60 by subtracting one standard deviation of 2.40 points from the mean of 22 points. Similarly, to obtain the value representing one standard deviation above the mean I added 2.40 to the mean of 22 and obtain 24.40. Again, 68% of scores fall between plus and minus one standard deviation from the mean. In our example, the mean is 22 and one standard deviation equals 2.40 points.

The standard deviation can be obtained from most spreadsheet programs. Statistical consultants can provide the means and standard deviations for your survey items or groups of items. Recall that with some values it is better to think of the median and range instead of the mean and standard deviation.

Describing Relationships

If our survey contains items that represent two or more sets of items, we can examine relationships among the data. For example, we can look at the relationship between years of marriage and marital satisfaction. The statistic that represents the relationship is known as a correlation coefficient. A common correlation coefficient is known as the Pearson r. The value of r ranges from -1.0 to + 1.0.

The value of r tells us two things about a relationship. The size of the value indicates the strength of the relationship. A relationship of -1.0 and +1.0 represent equally strong and perfect relationships. Perfect relationships do not occur in research but some relationships are strong enough to be above .90. Relationships of - .75 and +.75 are equally strong and indicate a strong relationship between two measures. The positive and negative signs tell us the direction of the relationship. We usually do not include the positive sign. If r = .75 for the relationship between years of marriage and marital satisfaction then we know that for our sample, the longer people are married the more likely they will have higher satisfaction scores than people who have been married only a few years.

In contrast, if r = -.75 for the relationship between years of marriage and marital satisfaction then we know that for our sample, the longer people are married the more likely they will have lower satisfaction scores than people who have been married many years. The negative sign indicates an inverse relationship between years of marriage and marital satisfaction.

Because items like years of marriage and scores on marital satisfaction can vary, researchers refer to them as variables. The correlation coefficient is a measure of covariation. Said another way, the r value tells us two things about how any two variables co-vary. We know if they vary in the same or opposite directions and the size of the r value tells us the strength of the covariation.

Analyzing Differences

If our survey includes items that allow us to consider subgroups of participants then we can examine scores for groups of people and determine to what extent they are similar or different. For example, if we were to include items to measure forgiveness in a survey at the end of a seminar, we may want to know if there was a difference between people who were in the forgiveness seminar and those who did not attend (our comparison group).

In this example, seminar group is a variable that varies in two ways—participation in the seminar or not. Our second variable is a forgiveness score on the survey. The score on the survey can vary across a wide range if we have several items.

Here's an example of a forgiveness survey. In one study, I worked with two colleagues (Sutton, Jordan, & Worthington, 2014) to examine forgiveness and other variables in a religious sample. We used the *Trait Forgiveness Scale* (Berry et al., 2005) to measure forgiveness, which has a theoretical score range of 10 to 50. The scale has 10-items (e.g., "I am a forgiving person"). Each item has a five-point rating scale: 1 = *strongly disagree* to 5 = *strongly agree*. Thus, on a theoretical basis, a person could score a 10 if they answered all items as a 1 and someone else could score a 50 if they answered all 10 items as a 5. In case you wondered, the mean for our sample was 39.66 and the standard deviation was 6.17.

Statisticians can use various tests to determine if a difference between groups is statistically significant. A common test for two groups is called the *t*-test which looks at the difference between the means for each group. The statistical procedure results in a *t*-value and a *p* value. The larger the *t*-value, the more likely it is that the difference between the group means is significant. The *p*-value represents the probability that the *t*-value of the size obtained did not occur by chance. As in many cases, the *p*-value is reported based on a 95% probability that the *t*-value did not occur by chance. The *p*-value is usually reported by considering the likelihood that it occurs by chance greater or less than 5% of the time where 5% is written as .05. If the probability is less than .05 that a *t*-value as large or larger than the one obtained did not occur by chance, the researcher would report the results as $p < .05$. If the *t*-value was too small to meet the level needed for significance, the researcher would just report the finding as not significant ($p > .05$).

In our hypothetical forgiveness seminar study, suppose people who attended the seminar had higher forgiveness scores than those who did not attend and that the higher scores were statistically significant, which means the difference is reliable 95% of the time we would conduct a similar study. The researcher would report the means and standard deviations for each group along with the *t*-value and the *p*-value. It might look something like this. We found that people who did attended the forgiveness seminar were significantly more forgiving ($M = 39$, $SD = 5$) than were people who did not attend the seminar ($M = 30$, $SD = 5$), $t(98) = 6.75$, $p < .05$.

The *t* test is a relatively simple procedure to study differences between two-groups. A variety of other tests are available to examine differences among many groups. These procedures are covered in courses on statistics. Many of the tests can be performed using the statistical procedures in spreadsheets. Alternatively, a survey team may hire a statistical consultant to conduct the analyses and provide interpretive reports.

Summary

Many human characteristics conform to a normal or bell-shaped distribution.

In a normal distribution of scores, the mode, median, and mean all fall at the same location in the middle of the distribution.

When characteristics are normally distributed, we can know what percentage of people with those characteristics fall within one, two, and three standard deviations from average.

We can study the direction and strength of the relationship between two variables by calculating a Pearson *r* correlation coefficient.

The Pearson *r* values range from -1.0 to +1.0.

Positive values indicate that as one value increases or decreases, so does the other. Negative values indicate that as one value increases, the other value decreases.

The size of the Pearson *r* value indicates the strength of the relationship.

Statisticians can examine survey data to determine if scores for subgroups are significantly different. One example of a difference test is the *t*-test.

Concepts

Correlation coefficient
Normal curve
Pearson *r*
p value
Range
Standard deviation
t test

17. Assessing Survey Reliability

Objectives:
  Define reliability related to survey scores.
  State the range of a reliability statistic.
  Describe common methods of determining survey reliability.

The reliability of a survey actually refers to the reliability of the results because reliability is a property of the scores not the survey items. Statisticians can calculate reliability values for parts of a survey that result in a set of scored items. The values will indicate consistency or stability depending on the procedure. In this chapter, I will review common reliability statistics and methods.

Reliability statistics are reported for groups of items on surveys that cover a specific topic such as compassion, marriage satisfaction, or spiritual practices. The values range from 0.00 to 1.00 where higher numbers indicate high levels of reliability. Reliability values are always tied to a particular set of scores or values obtained in one sample. Every time a survey is used, a new reliability value is obtained, which is why it is not possible to say a survey questionnaire has a particular reliability value. We can only report values from its use in previous studies. Most well-written surveys of attitudes and beliefs yield reliability values in the range of .75 to .90. in general, longer surveys yield higher values because you are collecting more responses from your respondents.

Common Methods of Assessing Reliability

The vocabulary applicable to the reliability of surveys comes from research on testing so when I use a term like test-retest reliability, I am referring to a survey or a part of a survey as a test. By *part of a survey* I mean a subset of items that are focused on one specific topic. For example, in a 25-item survey about spiritual growth, there may be a subset of 5-items dealing with personal devotions and a different subset of 5-items about faith at work. We can think of the five items as a small test and calculate reliability statistics for the scores produced by respondents who completed those five items. We can do the same for other groups of items thus, even a small survey with 25 items may contain 4-5 groups of items having various reliability values.

Test-Retest Reliability
If we administer a survey about spiritual practices to a group of people today and again in two days, we can calculate a correlation coefficient for the two sets of scores. In general, we would expect reports of spiritual practices to be fairly stable over two days thus we would expect a high test-retest correlation coefficient such as $r_{tt} = .87$. The double t in the subscript indicates this reliability coefficient is a test-retest statistic.

You might suspect that time makes a difference. If you take the same achievement test twice within a one-week interval, you might remember some of the items and figure out the correct answer to the ones you missed. Scores can be higher when retesting achievement after a short period of time. Hope can vary a lot more than a skill such as reading comprehension. Hope can improve or worsen over time. We would not expect scores on a measure of hope to have high retest values over a period of months compared to a three-day interval.

Parallel, Equivalent, and Alternate Forms Reliability

Instead of giving the same survey twice, some researchers create two or more forms of a questionnaire that are supposed to yield similar scores. Although two sets of items may be similar, they are not exactly the same so a perfect correlation will not be possible. Having more than one form can be helpful to overcome problems of retesting with the same items. For example, you could use similar but slightly different gratitude surveys at the beginning and end of a gratitude workshop.

Internal Consistency Methods of Reliability

Methods of internal consistency calculate values based on score patterns on one administration of a survey. For example, a person with a high degree of compassion ought to score high on most items that measure compassion. Methods of internal consistency are useful because researchers can calculate values based on one administration of a survey. There are a few methods to calculate internal consistency.

Split-Half and Odd-Even Reliability

A simple method to calculate internal consistency is to divide survey items in half and calculate a correlation coefficient between the scores for the two halves. A common practice is to split the group of items based on even and odd numbered items.

A problem with this method is a reliable finding that shorter surveys generally produce less reliable scores than do longer surveys. A mathematical formula can be used to estimate the reliability value for a full set of items based on the value obtained from a split-half calculation. You will see this value referred to in test manuals as *Spearman-Brown*. To use the Spearman-Brown formula, multiply the split-half reliability by two and divide by one-plus the reliability value. For example, if the split-half reliability value for a leadership survey is .75 we multiple .75 by 2 to get 1.50 then divide 1.50 by 1.75 (1 + .75), which equals .86 (rounded).

Cronbach's Coefficient Alpha

In survey research, Cronbach's coefficient alpha is a commonly reported internal consistency statistic. This measure is sometimes just referred to as alpha or by the Greek letter alpha (α). Alpha represents the average correlation for each pair of items from one administration of a survey. Alpha is commonly used with rating items. For example, in one study I and two colleagues surveyed Christian counselors. We included items from the Intratextual Fundamentalism Scale (Williamson et al., 2010) to assess fundamentalist beliefs. The Cronbach's alpha value was .83 (Sutton et al., 2016).

Summary

Reliability is a property of the scores obtained from a survey and not the survey itself.

The values of a reliability coefficient range from 0.0 to 1.0.

Researchers commonly report the coefficient alpha reliability of scores from subsections of a survey.

For survey sections that are like tests used on a regular basis, researchers may report reliability values from different methods such as test-retest and alternate, equivalent, or parallel forms.

Concepts

Alternate Forms Reliability
Cronbach's Coefficient Alpha
Equivalent Forms Reliability
Internal Consistency Methods of Reliability
Odd-Even Reliability
Parallel Forms Reliability
Reliability
Spearman-Brown
Split-Half Reliability
Test-Retest Reliability

18. Assessing Survey Validity

Objectives:

Define validity related to survey results.
Describe common methods of assessing survey validity.

The validity of a survey refers to how well it accomplishes its purpose. As we have noted previously, surveys are designed to collect some information. A survey of leadership styles ought to collect information about at least two leadership styles. There is no single value or method that determines the validity of a survey. Instead, validity is a cumulative concept based on the findings of many studies. As with reliability, our focus is upon the validity of scores not the survey. Recall that scores associated with a survey vary every time we administer a survey. If the same survey is used several times, we can gain a sense of how well the items accomplish their intended purpose by examining the range of validity coefficients calculated for different samples.

     There is a relationship between reliability and validity. Researchers state that reliability is a necessary but not sufficient condition for validity. A survey may have a history of producing reliable scores—scores that are very stable and have a high degree of internal consistency. Although we may find survey scores were consistent and stable, the finding does not mean the survey scores accomplish their purpose. A survey about leadership styles may yield reliable findings but it would not tell us how leaders manage stress nor would be learn their attitudes toward social issues. Of course, you might also find that leaders disagree about what leadership behavior patterns ought to be measured to say we have actually measured leadership styles.

Basic Validity Concepts

Content Validity

When developing a survey, we write items we believe will gather information related to our topics of interest. If we construct a ten-item survey to evaluate a workshop on leadership, we must be sure that we are actually measuring the theoretical domain called leadership. We should begin by defining leadership and writing a variety of items that address the key components of our definition. After generating a list of potential items, we would want to get feedback from experts in the field of leadership studies. Alternatively, we might find a set of questions used in previous studies that we can use in our survey. Content validity refers to the degree to which our survey items are related to the purpose of the survey. We rely on informed judgment concerning the content. If we wish to define leadership in a specific way then we ought to have a specific definition. For example, instead of a general questionnaire about leadership, we might consider a few styles like democratic or authoritarian.

Criterion-Related Validity

Criterion-related validity compares a set of scores on one set of items to those from another set of items using a correlation procedure. A common correlation coefficient is the Pearson r to which an xy subscript is added to represent scores on two different sets of items. There are two types of criterion-related validity.

Concurrent Validity

Concurrent validity compares two sets of scores from a current study. In one study, I and some colleagues compared a set of forgiveness items with a set of compassion items. We expected a positive correlation because, although the two constructs are not the same, we would question the validity of our items if they were totally unrelated or even negatively correlated. It turns out, there was a significant positive correlation ($r_{xy} = .25$, $p < .01$) between the two different measures (Sutton et al., 2014).

Predictive Validity

Another type of criterion-related validity is predictive validity. In this type of validity, a set of scores are compared to a future criterion. For example, we may wish to see if an employer's ratings of leadership potential are a good predictor of job performance at the end of the first year of employment.

Construct Validity

Every characteristic or trait is a construct that includes a list of criteria. When we write about employee strengths, we refer to other constructs such as conscientiousness and integrity. Construct validity refers to a collection of evidence using different methods that support the existence of a particular construct, which can be recognized by many independent researchers. Support for a construct comes from various studies.

Judgment Analysis

Suppose employees complete a survey about their leadership qualities after being on the job for six months. At the same time, we have their supervisors evaluate the leadership qualities of their employees. We are now in a position to see how well the judgment of the supervisors matches the employees' survey responses. We would not expect a perfect match but if our employee survey is usually valid for measuring leadership qualities then the responses should be at least moderately correlated with the judgments of their supervisors.

You may be familiar with a similar problem in teaching. In my experience as a professor, I found many colleagues did not consider the course evaluations completed by students to be a valid measure of the courses they taught. Studies involving judgment analyses contribute to understanding construct validity.

Factor Analysis

Factor analysis is a mathematical strategy to analyze groups of items within a large survey to see how well they relate to each other. A common type of factor analysis is *principal components analysis*. For example, we may expect survey items that assess religious virtues like forgiveness and compassion to be highly correlated with the virtues they are supposed to measure but have lower correlations with virtues they were not supposed to measure. If we write five forgiveness items and five compassion items then we would hope to find the five forgiveness items are all highly correlated with forgiveness and not compassion. Likewise, we expect the five compassion items to be all highly correlated with compassion but not forgiveness. When researchers conduct factor analysis of surveys, they aim at explaining the structure of the survey. There are different types of factor analysis and different methods of calculating the factors.

Convergent Validity

Convergent validity can be assessed by comparing two different measures of the same construct. For example, there are several measures of forgiveness. If two surveys of forgiveness measure the same construct, the scores ought to result in a significant positive correlation. If the correlations are not high we may question which survey is the best measure of forgiveness. We may also wonder if each survey really examines only a part of the construct forgiveness. Thus, in addition to looking at the numbers, researchers must also consider the wording of items.

Discriminant Validity

Discriminant validity is like the opposite of convergent validity. In convergent validity, we expected to find a positive relationship between two measures of the same or similar constructs. In discriminant validity, we expect to find little or no relationship between dissimilar constructs. We would not expect a measure of courage to be significantly correlated with a measure of organizational skills. We would not expect high forgiveness scores to be positively correlated with high revenge scores. If two very different constructs produce high positive validity coefficients, we ought to challenge the validity. We may need to ask questions of respondents to figure out why two seemingly different constructs are highly related.

Multicultural Concerns

A survey that produces high validity values in one culture may not work so well in another culture even if two cultures use the same language. We know translating a survey from one language to another is not easy. We should also remember that culture is more than language. We should not assume that English speakers in Scotland hold the same attitudes as those in the

United States or Australia. We should not assume that Spanish speakers in Puerto Rico respond to items in the same way as people in New Mexico or Chile. Neither should we assume a survey that yields high validity values in one faith group will produce similar values in another group. A colleague, Rod Bassett of Roberts Wesleyan College in Rochester New York, told me of difficulties obtaining valid results using a survey of morality that had worked well in other samples but did not work well with the Christian student sample at his college.

Summary

Validity refers to how well the obtained responses support the purpose of a survey.

Validity is a property of an interpretation and the uses of scores, not surveys.

High reliability values are important to obtaining high validity values, but high reliability values do not guarantee high validity values.

Validity, associated with scores produced by a survey, is a broad concept based on the findings from many studies using different methods.

The content validity of a survey is based on the judgments of experts.

Several methods of determining survey validity produce numerical values for example: factor analysis, concurrent and predictive validity, convergent and discriminant validity.

Construct validity emerges from a collection of evidence obtained from several studies using multiple methods.

Validity values obtained in one culture may not be the same in a different culture even if the language is the same or similar.

Concepts

Construct validity
Content validity
Concurrent validity
Convergent validity
Criterion-related validity
Discriminant validity
Factor analysis
Judgment analysis
Predictive validity
Principal components analysis
Validity

19. Presenting Results

Objectives:

Describe key features important to presenting survey results using tables.

Describe key features important to presenting survey results using charts.

The relative ease of creating tables and charts has increased our expectations about how data ought to be displayed. A well-designed table or chart provides useful information in a way that is more understandable than burying numbers in dense text. Of course, tables and charts can be confusing. My focus in this chapter is to describe a few simple ways to present the results of a survey to an educated audience. I do not intend to review the unique requirements of presenting data for publication in academic journals, which will vary with editorial style.

Tables

Tables can be used to summarize the responses for any group of data obtained from a survey. At a simple level, we can present the survey items along with the responses. At a more complex level, we can present the responses to groups of items based on subgroups such as age, sex, or organization.

Table 1

Table 1 is an example of a simple table Heather Kelly and I (Sutton & Kelly, 2015) used to present survey data about the Christian identity of counselors. You can create tables like this in spreadsheet, word processing, and presentation programs.

Table 1: Presentation Example

COUNSELORS: CHRISTIAN IDENTITY		
Identity	N	Percent
Catholic	8	3.2
Evangelical	82	32.7
Pentecostal/Charismatic	48	19.1
Nondenominational	43	17.1
Other	27	10.8
Not reporting	43	17.1

Table 2

Table 2 is an example of a simple table that includes an abbreviation of a statement in the left side column, the number of people (*n*) who responded, and three columns for percentages. The original question gave respondents a five-point choice from *Strongly agree* to *Strongly disagree*. For our slide presentation, we regrouped the responses. *Disagree* includes *Strongly disagree and Disagree,* the middle column remains the same as *Neither agreeing or disagreeing,* and the final column is a regrouping of the options for *Agree and Strongly agree.*

If you were including a table like this in a report, it would be important to include more details in the table. For example, you could present the table in a landscape format including the original items and all five response columns (*Strongly disagree* to *Strongly agree*). Also, since the number of people is similar, you could provide the "*n*" in a note below the table.

Table 2: Beliefs of Christian Counselors about Social Issues

Social Issue	n	Disagree %	Neither %	Agree %
Abortion: Always sinful	212	34.91	17.45	47.64
Abortion: ok risk of harm	212	17.45	26.89	55.19
Abortion: ok rape/ incest	213	47.89	29.11	23.00

Guidelines for Tables in Reports

- Create tables to replace lengthy and dense presentations of results in paragraphs.
- Number each table.
- Provide a short descriptive title for each table.
- Clearly label all columns.
- Include all the information in the table that readers need in order to understand the table.
- Simplify tables by placing similar information in a note below the table.
- Maintain a consistent reporting of abbreviations and statistical values in all tables.
- Include notes below the table to explain special abbreviations or symbols.
- Only omit explanatory notes for commonly used symbols (e.g., %, $) and abbreviations (e.g., U.S., A.M., lb.).
- In the text of the report, refer to each table by number.

If you are writing an academic paper, be sure to follow the guidelines in your discipline. Journal editors publish guidelines for authors. If you are producing tables for a course instructor, be sure to follow their guidelines. Experience indicates that instructors may have unique preferences. For example, although most psychology instructors follow APA style, some want the tables and figures in the report in contrast to the usual placement at the end of an article prepared for publication.

Guidelines for Tables in Presentations
- Keep tables simple and use fonts large enough to read from the back of the room.
- Explain pertinent details as you present the table to the audience.
- Ensure that use of color enhances the clarity of the presentation. Some colors do not project well and can make text difficult to read.
- Ask for peer feedback before you present to a large audience.

Charts
Graphical displays of data are common in media reports of surveys. A chart is the generic name for a visual presentation of data. Spreadsheets and statistical software programs include a variety of charts. I will review a few commonly used charts. The term *figure* refers to any graphical object prepared for publication. Journal editors provide authors with specific guidelines for including figures in their articles. Figures can include charts, drawings, and photos. The fonts within figures may be smaller than those permitted in reports.

Clustered Column Charts

These charts are useful for displaying percentages. Chart 1 is an example of a chart displaying reports of daily prayer practice by men and women for a fictitious sample.

Chart 1: Clustered Column Chart

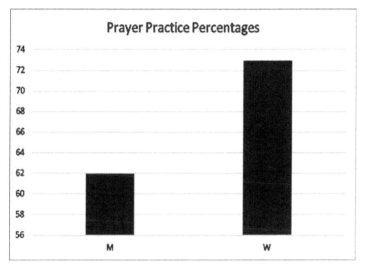

Pie Charts

Pie charts are useful for displaying data that are percentages or proportions. For readability, it is usually best to limit slices to six categories.

Chart 2 is an example of a pie chart illustrating Christian Identity for a fictitious sample. The percentages of people are shown as parts of the pie. The legend to the right explains the shaded regions. This is an example of when color would be more useful than shades of gray.

Chart 2: Christian Identity for the sample.

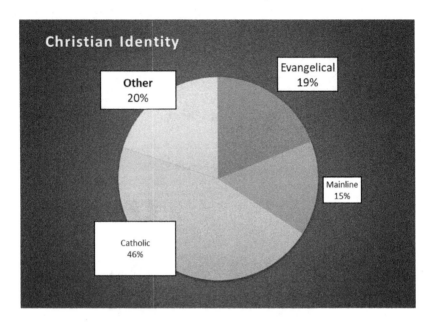

Line Charts

Line charts are useful for tracking changes in data across time.

Chart 3: Millions of dollars donated by quarter and year.

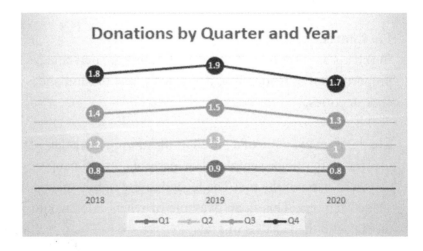

Chart 3 is an example showing dollars donated for each quarter of a year over a three-year period. Different shades of gray are used for the quarters and the dollars are shown in circles. Again, it would be best to use colors if available. As with other charts, you will need to explain the values.

Guidelines for Charts in Reports

- Use charts to support or simplify data in a report.
- Number the charts in the order presented.
- Provide a short descriptive title for each chart.
- Make sure the fonts in charts are large enough to read. For example, avoid fonts lower than 8-point.
- Label the horizontal and vertical axes when using graphs
- Include brief captions as needed for explanation.

Guidelines for Charts in Presentations

- Keep charts simple and use fonts large enough to read from the back of the room.
- Explain pertinent details as you present the chart to the audience.
- Ensure that use of color enhances the clarity of the presentation.
- Ask for peer feedback before you present.

Summary

Research teams have many options for presenting data to an audience.

Tables can simplify the presentation of grouped data using rows and columns.

Charts can be used to compare different categories of data at one point in time or across time.

Concepts

Figure
Clustered column chart
Legend
Line chart
Pie chart
Table

References

Alonso-Arbiol, Itziar, van de Vijver, Fons J. R., Fernandez, Itziar, Paez, Dario, Campos, Miryam, & Carrera, Pilar. (2011). Implicit theories about interrelations of anger components in 25 countries. *Emotion, 11*, 1-11. doi: 10.1037/a0020295

Antonuccio D.O., Danton W.G., & McClanahan T.M. (2003). Psychology in the prescription era: building a firewall between marketing and science. *American Psychologist, 58*, 1028-43. doi: https://doi.org/10.1037/0003-066X.58.12.1028

Asch, S. E. (1946). Forming impressions of personality. *The Journal of Abnormal and Social Psychology, 41*, 258-290. doi:10.1037/h0055756

Berry, J. W., Worthington, E. R., O'Connor, L. E., Parrott, L., & Wade, N. G. (2005). Forgivingness, vengeful rumination, and affective traits. *Journal of Personality, 73*, 183-225. doi:10.1111/j.1467-6494.2004.00308.x

Burnes, B., & Cooke, B. (2013). Kurt Lewin's field theory: A review and re-evaluation. *International Journal of Management Reviews, 15*, 408-425.

Bycio, Peter, Hackett, Rick D., & Allen, Joyce S. (1995). Further assessments of Bass's (1985) conceptualization of transactional and transformational leadership. *Journal of Applied Psychology, 80*, 468-478. doi: 10.1037/0021-9010.80.4.468

Cialdini, R. B. (2003) "Crafting normative messages to protect the environment." *Current directions in psychological science*, *12*, 105-109.

Choma, B. L., Haji, R., Hodson, G., & Hoffarth, M. (2016). Avoiding cultural contamination: Intergroup disgust sensitivity and religious identification as predictors of interfaith threat, faith-based policies, and islamophobia. *Personality and Individual Differences*, *95*, 50-55. doi: 10.1016/j.paid.2016.02.013

D'Souza, R. (2007). The importance of spirituality in medicine and its application to clinical practice. *Medical Journal of Australia, 186*, S57.

De Hoogh, A. H. B., Den Hartog, D. N., Koopman, P. L., Thierry, H., Van den Berg, P. T., Van der Weide, J. G., & Wilderom, C. P. M. (2005). Leader motives, charismatic leadership, and subordinates' work attitude in the profit and voluntary sector. *The Leadership Quarterly, 16*, 17-38. doi: 10.1016/j.leaqua.2004.10.001

Dwiwardani, C., Hill, P. C., Bollinger, R. A., Marks, L. E., Steele, J. R., Doolin, H. N., . . . Davis, D. E. (2014). Virtues develop from a secure base: Attachment and resilience as predictors of humility, gratitude, and forgiveness. *Journal of Psychology and Theology, 42*, 83-90.

Farley, S. D. & Stasson, M. F. (2003). Relative influences of affect and cognition on behavior: Are feelings or beliefs more related to blood donation intentions? *Experimental Psychology, 50,* 53-62. doi: 10.1027//1618-3169.50.1.55

Funk, J. L., & Rogge, R. D. (2007). Testing the ruler with item response theory: Increasing precision of measurement for relationship satisfaction with the Couples Satisfaction Index. *Journal of Family Psychology, 21,* 572–583.

Gosling, S.D., Ko, S.J., Mannarelli, T., Morris, M.E. (2002). A room with a cue: Personality judgments based on offices and bedrooms. *Journal of Personality and Social Psychology, 82,* 379-398.

Graham, J. M., Diebels, K.J., & Barnow, Z. B. (2011). The reliability of relationship satisfaction: A reliability generalization meta-analysis. *Journal of Family Psychology, 25,* 39-48.

Jackson, L. A., Hodge, C. N., Gerard, D. A., Ingram, J. M., Ervin, K.S., & Sheppard, L.A. (1996). Cognition, affect, and behavior in the prediction of group attitudes. *Personality and Social Psychology Bulletin, 22,* 306-316. doi: 10.1177/0146167296223009

Koenig, H. G., Meador, K., & Parkerson, G. (1997). Religion Index for Psychiatric Research: A 5-item measure for use in health outcome studies [Letter to the editor]. *The American Journal of Psychiatry, 154,* 885-886.

Lazarus, A. A. (1989). *The Practice of Multimodal Therapy: Systematic, Comprehensive, and Effective Psychotherapy*. Baltimore: Johns Hopkins University Press.

Littman-Ovadia, H. & Lavy, S. (2015). Going the extra mile: Perseverance as a key character strength at work. *Journal of Career Assessment, 24*, 240-252.

Livingston, G. et al. (2017). Dementia prevention, intervention, and care. *The Lancet*, online first. Doi: http://dx.doi.org/10.1016/S0140-6736(17)31363-6

Locke, H. J., & Wallace, K. M. (1959). Short marital adjustment and prediction tests: Their reliability and validity. *Marriage and Family Living, 21*, 251–255.

Lyubomirsky, S., & Lepper, H. S. (1999). A measure of subjective happiness: Preliminary reliability and construct validation. *Social Indicators Research, 46*, 137-155. doi: 10.1023/A:1006824100041

Marigold, D. C., Cavallo, J. V., Holmes, J. G., & Wood, J. V. (2014). You can't always give what you want: The challenge of providing social support to low self-esteem individuals. *Journal of Personality and Social Psychology, 107*, 56-80. doi: 10.1037/a0036554

McCullough, M. E., Emmons, R. A., & Tsang, J. (2002). The Grateful Disposition: A conceptual and Empirical Topography. *Journal of Personality and Social Psychology, 82*, 112-127.

McLeland, K. C., & Sutton, G. W. (2005) Military service, marital status, and men's relationship satisfaction. *Individual Differences Research, 3, 177-182.*

Mendelson, M. J. & Aboud, F. (1999). Measuring friendship quality in late adolescents and young adults: McGill friendship questionnaires. *Canadian Journal of Behavioural Science, 31,* 130-132.

Miller, G. A. (1996). How we think about cognition, emotion, and biology in psychopathology. *Psychophysiology, 33,* 615–628. doi:10.1111/j.1469-8986.1996.tb02356.x

Mostert, J. & Sutton, G.W. (2015, April). *Assessing spiritual growth and development in Christian communities.* Paper presented at the annual meeting of the Christian Association for Psychological Studies, International Conference, Denver, Colorado.

Nauts, S., Langner, O., Huijsmans, I., Vonk, R., & Wigboldus, D. J. (2014). Forming impressions of personality: A replication and review of Asch's (1946) evidence for a primacy-of-warmth effect in impression formation. *Social   Psychology, 45*(3),   153-163. doi:10.1027/1864-9335/a000179

Neider, L. L., & Schriesheim, C. A. (2011). The authentic leadership inventory (ALI): Development and empirical tests. *The Leadership Quarterly, 22,* 1146-1164. doi: 10.1016/j.leaqua.2011.09.008

Pargament, K.I., Koenig, H.G., & Perez, L. (2000). The many methods of religious coping: Initial development and validation of the RCOPE. *Journal of Clinical Psychology, 56,* 519-543.

Plante, T.J. & Boccaccini, B.F. (1997). The Santa Clara Strength of Religious Faith Questionnaire, *Pastoral Psychology, 45,* 375-387.

Plante, T.G., Vallaeys, C.L., Sherman, A.C., & Wallston, K.A. (2002). The development of a brief version of the Santa Clara Strength of Religious Faith Questionnaire. *Pastoral Psychology, 48,* 11-21.

Pop, J. L., Sutton, G.W., & Jones, E.G. (2009). Restoring pastors following a moral failure: The effects of self-interest and group influence, *Pastoral Psychology, 57,* 275-284.

Pritchett, R., Kemp, J., Wilson, P., Minnis, H., Bryce, G., & Gillberg, C. (2011). Quick, simple measures of family relationships for use in clinical practice and research. A systematic review. *Family Practice, 28,* 172-187. doi: https://doi.org/10.1093/fampra/cmq080

Roberts, B. W., Kuncel, N. R., Shiner, R., Caspi, A., & Goldberg, L. R. (2007). The power of personality. *Perspectives on Psychological Science, 2,* 313-345.

Sand-Jecklin, K., & Coyle, S. (2014). Efficiently assessing patient health literacy: The BHLS instrument. *Clinical*

Nursing   Research,   23,   581-600.   doi: 10.1177/1054773813488417

Schirmer, A. (2015). *Emotion.* Washington, DC: Sage.

Schumm, W. R., Paff-Bergen, L. A., Hatch, R. C., Obiorah, F. C., Copeland, J. M., Meens, L. D., & Bugaighis, M. A. (1986). Concurrent and discriminant validity of the Kansas Marital Satisfaction scale. *Journal of Marriage and the Family, 48,* 381-387.

Snyder, C. R., Harris, C., Anderson, J. R., Holleran, S. A., Irving, L. M., Sigmon, S. T., et al. (1991). The will and the ways: Development and validation of an individual-differences measure of hope. *Journal of Personality and Social Psychology, 60,* 570-585.

Sutton, G. W. (2016). *A house divided: Sexuality, morality, and Christian cultures.* Eugene, OR: Pickwick.

Sutton, G. W., Arnzen, C., & Kelly, H. (2016). Christian counseling and psychotherapy: Components of clinician spirituality that predict type of Christian intervention. *Journal of Psychology and Christianity, 35,* 204-214.

Sutton, G. W., Jordan, K., & Worthington, E.L., Jr. (2014). Spirituality, hope, compassion, and forgiveness: Contributions of Pentecostal spirituality to godly love. *Journal of Psychology and Christianity, 33,* 212-226

Sutton, G. W. & Kelly, H. (2015, September). *Assessment of Evidenced Based Christian Counseling.* Paper presented at the 2015 World Conference of the American Association of Christian Counseling, Nashville, TN.

Swisher, M. V. (1988). Similarities and differences between spoken languages and natural sign languages. *Applied Linguistics, 9,* 343-356. doi 10.1093/applin/9.4.343

Taylor, S., & Rachman, S. J. (1992). Fear and avoidance of aversive affective states: Dimensions and causal relations. *Journal of Anxiety Disorders, 6,* 15-25. doi: 10.1016/0887-6185(92)90022-Y

Watson, D. Clark, L.A. & Tellegen, A. (1988). Development and Validation of Brief Measures of Positive and Negative Affect: The PANAS Scales. *Journal of Personality and Social Psychology, 54,* 1063-1070.

Wilkinson, R. B. (2008). Development and properties of the Adolescent Friendship Attachment Scale. *Journal of Youth and Adolescence, 37*(10), 1270-1279. doi:10.1007/s10964-006-9141-7

Williamson, W.P., Hood, R. W. Jr., Ahmad, A., Sadiq, M., Y Hill, P.C. (2010). The intratextual fundamentalism scale: cross-cultural application, validity evidence, and relationship with religious orientation and the Big 5 factor markers. *Mental Health, Religion & Culture, 13,* 721-747.

Wilmoth, J.D. & Smyser, S. (2012). A national survey of marriage preparation provided by clergy. *Journal of Couple & Relationship Therapy, 11*, 69-85.

Wilt, J., & Revelle, W. (2015). Affect, behavior, cognition, and desire in the Big Five: An analysis of item content and structure. *European Journal of Personality, 29*, 478–497. http://doi.org/10.1002/per.2002

Worthington, E. L. Jr. (2006). *Forgiving and reconciliation: Theory and application.* New York: Routledge.

Worthington, E. L. Jr. (2003). *Forgiving and reconciling: Bridges to wholeness and hope.* Westmont, IL: Inter-Varsity.

Worthington, E.L., Jr., Wade, N.G., Hight, T.L., Ripley, J.S., McCullough, M.E., Berry, J.W. et al. (2003). The Religious Commitment Inventory—10: development, refinement, and validation of a brief scale for research and counseling. *Journal of Counseling and Psychology, 50*, 84-96.

Worthington, E. J., Witvliet, C. O., Pietrini, P., & Miller, A. J. (2007). Forgiveness, health, and well-being: A review of evidence for emotional versus decisional forgiveness, dispositional forgivingness, and reduced unforgiveness. *Journal of Behavioral Medicine, 30,* 291-302. doi:10.1007/s10865-007-9105-8

Research Vocabulary

I included additional terms to help reading some research terms even though they were not covered, or only briefly mentioned, in this book.

Abstract. A brief description of the contents of an article. Abstracts for research studies include the purpose, procedures, and key results.

Alpha (α). The probability of rejecting a true null hypothesis. Alpha also refers to a measure of internal consistency—see Cronbach's coefficient alpha.

Anchors. Words at each end of a rating scale indicate the extreme values such as *strongly disagree* and *strongly agree*.

Alternate forms reliability. A procedure for obtaining evidence of the reliability of test scores by calculating a reliability coefficient from scores produced by two or more forms of the same test. This is also known as Equivalent Forms Reliability. When there are two forms, the term Parallel Forms is sometimes used.

ANOVA. Analysis of Variance is a statistical procedure that analyzes variance between the means of the groups in a study compared to the variance among the participants in a study.

ANCOVA. Analysis of Covariance is a statistical procedure for analyzing results when there are one or more independent variables, one dependent variable, and one or more covariates.

APA style. A style of writing developed by the American Psychological Association, which is commonly used in journals reporting survey research.

Applied research. The use of research findings to improve society.

Archive. Data that has been stored and the location of the data.

Archival research. Studying data that has already been collected.

Bar graph. A figure that presents frequency data for categorical or discrete variables.

Basic research. Research conducted to advance knowledge in a discipline. Basic research may not have immediate applications.

Big Five. A set of personality traits widely researched in psychology. They include openness, conscientiousness, extroversion, agreeableness, and neuroticism. Neuroticism is sometimes referred to by the positive dimension of emotional stability.

Case studies. Detailed studies of one person or organization.

Categorical variable. Categorical variables are discrete variables having two or more groups or levels such as leadership style, ethnicity, and Protestant denomination.

Census. An official count or survey of a population.

Central tendency. Scores typical of a distribution such as mode, median, mean.

Chi-Square. A statistic that represents differences between obtained and expected values. The chi-square statistic can be used with frequency data. Chi square tests are nonparametric tests.

Closed-end items or questions. Survey items that limit responses to options provided by the item writer.

Cluster analysis. A data analysis strategy that groups data into similar categories or clusters.

Clustered column chart. A bar graph that displays data using vertical bars.

Cluster sample. A sample formed by identifying natural or existing groups (i.e., clusters like schools, organizations, churches) then sampling all persons within the group.

Coefficient alpha. See Cronbach's alpha.

Cognition. The dimension of human functioning dealing with thinking.

Cohen's *d*. An estimate of effect size often used with a *t* test.

Concurrent validity. A method to assess the validity of survey data based on the correlation of two sets of scores obtained at the same time.

Confidence interval. A range of values within which a value or score is likely to fall a specified percentage of the time a study is performed.

Confidence level. The probability that a value falls within a confidence interval. In survey research, common confidence levels are 95% and 99%.

Confidentiality. Limiting disclosure of collected information based on the participation agreement.

Confounding variable. A variable that produces unexpected changes in a dependent variable and therefore interferes with interpreting the influence of an independent variable on a dependent variable.

Construct. An idea defined by features that can be measured such as leadership, forgiveness, and hope.

Construct validity. Construct validity refers to the collection of evidence using different methods that support the existence of a particular construct.

Content validity. Content validity is the extent to which the items in a survey are judged by experts to adequately sample the domain a survey is supposed to assess.

Continuous variable. Continuous variables are those variables having a wide range of numerical values such as age, achievement, and personality.

Control group. The group in a study that does not receive an intervention or activity thought to produce a change.

Convenience sample. A sample composed of people who are willing and available to be in a study.

Correlation. Correlation refers to the relationship between two variables. When two variables vary in a specific way, they are said to covary.

Correlation coefficient. A statistic that summarizes a correlation between two variables. Correlations range from -1.0 to +1.0. Positive correlation values represent relationships that as one variable increases, so does the other. Negative correlation values represent relationships that are inverse. In an inverse relationship, one value increases as the other value decreases. A common coefficient is the Pearson Product Moment Correlation Coefficient reported using a lower case, italicized letter *r*. See also correlation.

Correlational research. Nonexperimental studies that examine relationships between variables.

Covariate. A variable that is correlated with a dependent variable.

Cramer's V. A correlation coefficient that may be used with nominal data.

Criterion related validity. Criterion-related validity compares a set of scores on one survey to scores on another survey using a correlation procedure.

Cronbach's Coefficient alpha. A statistic indicating the internal consistency of survey items based on an average of the interitem correlations in a sample.

Cross-sectional study. A survey of different ages of people completed at one point in time.

Data. In survey research, the data are the responses to survey items. Data may be numerical or text. Data is the plural of datum and takes a plural verb (e.g., data are).

Datum. A single unit of information, one response on a survey.

Debrief. To inform the participants of a study about the purpose of the study.

Demographics. Characteristics of human populations such as age, sex, and income.

Dependent groups design. Experimental designs which assign the same participants or matched pairs to the groups in a study.

Dependent variable (DV). The variable in a research study that is expected to change when a researcher varies the level of an independent variable.

Descriptive research. Research that describes characteristics of people and is not focused on testing hypotheses.

Descriptive statistics. Numerical values that summarize data obtained from samples. Examples of such statistics are mean, median, mode, standard deviation, range, and frequency distributions.

Discriminant Function Analysis. Discriminant function analysis is used to identify the relative contribution of variables to predict or explain a categorical outcome.

Effect size (*ES*). In general, an effect size is the size of the relationship between two variables. In experiments, effect size indicates how much of the variance in the dependent variable is accounted for by the independent variable. There are different measures of effect size such as Cohen's d, r^2 and eta-squared.

Eta-squared. A measure of treatment effect. An effect size.

Equivalent forms reliability. See alternate forms reliability.

Experiment. In the strict sense of the term, an experiment is a study of the effect of one or more independent variables on a dependent variable. Other variables are controlled by randomization using a control group. Experiments are usually designed to study cause-effect relationships.

External validity. The degree to which a research finding may be generalized to people or situations that were not explicitly studied.

Extraneous variable. A variable in a study that is not supposed to produce a change in a dependent variable. Variations in the noise level and staffing at a survey site are examples of extraneous variables.

F **test**. Sometimes used to refer to an ANOVA. A statistical test of differences between means.

Face-to-face interview. An interview conducted in person.

Face validity. A term for the way a survey or test appears valid to a respondent or participant. Face validity is not a technical dimension of validity and is sometimes confused with content validity.

Factor Analysis. Factor analysis is a statistical strategy using correlations to discover patterns of relationships among many variables in a large database.

Field research. Research conducted in natural settings in contrast to research labs or artificially created situations.

Field theory. A theory developed by Kurt Lewin, which in part posited that human behavior was a function of the person and the environment.

Focus group. A group of people brought together to respond to prepared questions. They may also complete surveys.

Frequency. The number of times a response is made. For example, the number of times respondents chose *Strongly agree* as their response to a survey item.

Hawthorne Effect. A finding that people change when they know they are being studied.

Gender. The socially defined characteristics expected of people in different cultures who have particular biological sex characteristics.

Goodness-of-fit test. A chi-square test that compares obtained with expected frequencies.

Group-administered survey. Collecting data by administering a survey to a group of participants.

Histogram. A figure used to present frequency data for a continuous variable.

Hypothesis. A statement about how concepts are related or predicted to be related.

Hypothesis testing. Research conducted to assess the validity of a hypothesis.

Independent variable (IV). A variable in a research study thought to produce a change in the dependent variable.

Inferential statistics. Statistical procedures for drawing conclusions about a population based on samples.

Informed Consent. An agreement to participate in a survey or other research project granted by an adult or legal representative who has been properly informed about the purpose and procedures involved in taking a survey or participating in a research project.

Institutional Review Board (IRB). The group of people within an organization authorized to review and approve research projects.

Interaction effect. The effects on a dependent variable produced by a combination of levels of independent variables. In contrast to a main effect.

Internal validity. The degree to which changes in dependent variables can be attributed to changes in one or more independent variables.

Intersex. Intersex is a general term for people who are born with variations in physical sex characteristics that are not distinctively male or female. The variations may be in genitals, reproductive organs, and chromosomes.

Interrater agreement. Degree to which two or more raters agree in their ratings.

Interval scale. A measurement scale that has equal-sized intervals between values.

Interview. A survey method in which a researcher collects data by asking respondents questions instead of asking them to complete a survey form.

Inventory. A set of statements or questions used to collect information about people. A form of survey.

Item. In a survey, an item is an individual statement that calls for a response or a question.

Judgment analysis. A method of survey validity that considers the judgments of experts in a content area.

Kendall's tau. A correlation coefficient that indicates the relationship between sets of ordinal data.

Lifespace. Lewin's concept of the psychological field that includes a person's experiences and needs.

Likert scale. A research measure containing statements and asking people to indicate their response in a range of values such as from agreement to disagreement.

Line chart. A graph displaying data as points on a graph connected by line segments.

Linear relationship. A visual portrayal of a relationship between two variables that can be described by a straight line.

Literature review. An article that organizes, summarizes, integrates, and critically evaluates research on a specific topic.

Research articles contain brief literature reviews relevant to the current study.

Logistic Regression. Logistic Regression is a statistical procedure used to predict an outcome that has two or more categories.

Longitudinal research. Studying the same people over time e.g., at different life stages.

Main effects. The effects of each independent variable on a dependent variable in ANOVA. See also interaction effect.

MANOVA. Multivariate Analysis of Variance. A statistical procedure for analyzing results when there are one or more independent variables and two or more dependent variables.

MANCOVA. Multivariate Analysis of Variance. A statistical procedure for analyzing results when there are one or more independent variables and two or more dependent variables, and one or more covariates.

Manuscript. The form of an article sent to publishers for consideration. Most publishers request double-spaced manuscripts with tables and figures at the end of the document or in separate files.

Matched groups design. An experimental design where participants are matched or made equivalent on one or more variables that are correlated with the dependent variable.

Matching variable. A variable in a matched groups design that is correlated with the dependent variable.

Mean. The arithmetic average for a set of scores or values.

Measure. A generic term for ways to measure responses in research. Measures include surveys, single-item ratings, and published tests.

Median. The number representing the mid-point in a set of scores or values. The median divides a distribution of scores in half. Half the scores are above the median and half the scores are below the median.

Mediating variable. A variable that is both predicted by an independent variable and predicts a dependent variable.

Meta-analysis. Research that examines the relationship between variables based on results of many studies.

Mode. The number representing the most frequent score in a distribution of scores. A distribution may have more than one mode.

Moderating variables. Variables in a study that have the effect of increasing, decreasing, or even reversing the effects of an independent variable on a dependent variable.

Multiple Regression. Multiple Regression refers to regression procedures in which several predictor variables are used to predict one criterion variable.

Naturalistic observation. Observing behavior of people in their natural settings.

Negative correlation. An inverse relationship between two variables.

Nominal scale. A scale that uses numbers to identify categories.

Null hypothesis. This is the assumption of no difference between the means stated in terms of population values on the dependent variable. Most researchers only report the research question or research hypothesis and rarely state the null hypothesis. Example: There is no difference between the population means of regular and special education teacher's job satisfaction scores.

Odd-even reliability. See split-half reliability.

Open-ended questions. Questions that permit respondents to create their own answers.

Ordinal scale. A scale of values where the numbers indicate differences in order or ranking but the intervals between the values may not be equal.

Parallel forms reliability. See Alternate Forms reliability.

Pearson Product Moment Correlation coefficient. See correlation coefficient.

Phi coefficient. An effect size sometimes reported with chi-square analyses.

Pie chart. A graph showing a circle divided into sections representing a portion of the whole.

Poll. A survey.

Population. The entire group of people who have the characteristics important to a particular study.

Predictive validity. A type of criterion-related validity. A procedure that relies on knowledge about the correlation between two sets of score data to predict future scores or values from the results of a current set of scores or data. For example, predicting future college GPA from knowledge of the relationship between a high school aptitude test and college GPA in previous studies.

Principal components analysis. A form of factor analysis that attempts to group many items in a survey into a smaller number of principal or main components.

Probability (p). The probability of falsely rejecting the null hypothesis. The p value is commonly compared to an alpha level. Common values are .05 and .01 depending on the nature of the variables and the research questions.

Program evaluation. Research designed to evaluate the extent to which programs meet their purposes, goals, and objectives.

Questionnaire. A survey. An organized set of statements or questions.

Random assignment. Forming research groups by randomly assigning members of a sample to different groups in a study.

Random sampling. Forming a sample of people who have an equal probability of being included in the sample.

Range. The span of a distribution of values or scores.

Rating scales. Scales used in surveys to assign numerical values to a range of responses.

Ratio scale. Scales that have equal-sized intervals and a true zero point.

Referral sampling. A type of convenience sample where respondents are referred by others.

Reliability (survey). The degree of stability or consistency associated with scores obtained from using a specific survey.

Regression. Regression is a statistical procedure used to predict values on a *criterion* variable from the knowledge of values obtained on a *predictor* variable.

Research hypothesis. A statement about the expected relationship between variables in a study.

Respondent. A person who completes a survey. Respondents may be called participants in research studies. In old articles, they were called subjects.

Response set. A tendency of respondents to answer all survey items the same way.

Sample. A small set of data drawn from a large set of data called the population. A population is the entire set of data.

Sampling frame. A list of the people in a population.

SCOPES model. Sutton's organization of human functioning as five dimensions (Cognition, Observable behavior, Physiology, Emotion, Spirituality) within a Social context marked by an individual's time and life spaces.

Sex. In research, sex refers to biological characteristics of respondents such as male, female, or intersex. Sex is different from gender.

Scale. A measure of a characteristic that results in a number e.g., a hope scale or belief scale.

Script. In research, a script is a detailed set of procedures that researchers use to maintain a constant presentation of materials such as delivering the same workshop to all participants regardless of who leads the workshop.

Social desirability. The tendency of most people to answer surveys in ways that make them look good.

Spearman's Rank Order Correlation Coefficient. The Spearman Rank Order Correlation Coefficient indicates the relationship between sets of ordinal data.

Split-half method. A method of estimating the internal reliability of test scores by correlating two halves of a test. Often the test is split based on odd and even number items thus, it is sometimes called odd-even reliability.

Standard deviation (*SD*). A statistic based on the deviation of scores from their group mean. The number reveals how much the scores in a distribution deviate from the mean.

Standard Error of Estimate (SEE). A measure of error used to create a range above and below an estimated or predicted value or score. SEE is an indicator of precision in estimating values.

Standard Error of the Mean (SE, *se*). A measure of error used to create a range above and below an obtained sample mean suggesting where a mean might fall if means were calculated for repeated samples.

Standard Error of Measurement (SEM). A measure of error used to create a score range above and below an obtained test score suggesting where a person's true score might fall if the test were taken again. SEM is related to the reliability of test scores.

Stratified Random Samples. Samples formed by grouping people by characteristics called *strata* before taking a random sample.

Structural Equation Modeling. Structural Equation Modeling, known as *SEM*, is a complex approach to testing relationships among variables in a theoretical model.

Survey. A coherent collection of questions and statements designed to collect information such as opinions, beliefs, attitudes, and knowledge.

Systematic sample. A sample formed by selecting every nth person from a population.

Test. A set of questions or items used to collect information. In education and psychology, tests usually refer to formal assessments of knowledge, personality, and other variables.

***t*-test value**. A statistic reported when analyzing differences between the survey means from two groups.

Test-retest reliability. A method of calculating the reliability of survey scores based on giving the same survey or alternate forms separated by a period of time.

Validity (survey). The degree to which survey results support the purpose for which a survey was designed. There are different types of validity.

Variable. A variable is a characteristic that varies in two or more ways.

Variance (VAR). The variance is a measure of variability used in statistical analyses.

APPENDICES

Appendix A: Survey Approval Checklist

Appendix B: Online Ethics Resources

Appendix C: Survey Consent Example

Appendix D: Survey Debriefing Example

Appendix E: Organizing a Spreadsheet

Appendix F: Examples of Survey Items

Appendix G: Sample Workshop Evaluation

Appendix A
Survey Approval Checklist

This checklist is designed to offer guidance to leaders in organizations who are responsible to authorize qualified researchers to conduct a survey in their organization. It is not meant to be exhaustive. For example, your organization, professional association, or government may have other requirements regulating research.

Place a checkmark next to all items that have been answered to your satisfaction. If an item does not apply, mark it NA.

___ The survey title is clear and not misleading.
___ There is evidence of review board approval.
___ The survey does not violate any laws or organizational policies.
___ The age of participants is appropriate for our organization.
___ The procedures for informed consent are present.
___ If the survey is for minors, provision is included to gain consent from legal guardians and assent from minors.
___ The purpose of the survey is clearly stated.
___ The purpose of the survey is appropriate to our organization.
___ The survey procedures are clearly stated.
___ The estimated time length is clear and appropriate.
___ Any sensitive items are appropriate for our organization.
___ Questions about age, sex, gender, ethnicity, etc. are consistent with the values of our organization.
___ The statement of risks seems reasonable.
___ The statement of benefits seems reasonable.
___ The procedure to ensure confidentiality is adequate.

__ The procedure to decline or withdraw from participation in the survey is clear.

__ Information about who to contact is adequate (e.g., names, phone numbers, emails).

__ Information about how to get the results of the survey is clearly stated.

__ Information about incentives, if any, is clearly stated.

Appendix B
Online Ethics Resources

Depending on the type of research you plan, one or more of the following links may help answer ethical questions.

American Association of Pastoral Counselors https://www.socialworkers.org/pubs/code/default.asp

American Counseling Association ethics. http://www.counseling.org/knowledge-center/ethics

American Educational Research Association research ethics http://www.aera.net/About-AERA/AERA-Rules-Policies/Professional-Ethics

American Psychological Association ethical principles http://www.apa.org/ethics/code/

Association of Professional Chaplains http://www.professionalchaplains.org/content.asp?pl=198&contentid=199

American Sociological Association ethics http://www.asanet.org/membership/code-ethics

National Association of Social Workers ethics https://www.socialworkers.org/pubs/code/default.asp

Spiritual Care Professionals—link to a common code of ethics for several professionals. http://www.professionalchaplains.org/content.asp?pl=198&contentid=199

Here is a link to a blog post on survey ethics for online surveys: https://www.qualtrics.com/blog/ethical-issues-for-online-sur-veys/

Here is a link to the US Office for Human Research Protec-tions. https://www.hhs.gov/ohrp/

Following is a link to ethical guidelines for research involving human subjects published by the US National Institutes of Health. https://humansubjects.nih.gov/ethical-guidelines-reg-ulations

This link is to the National Science Foundation page on Re-sponsible Conduct of Research.
https://www.nsf.gov/bfa/dias/policy/rcr.jsp

Appendix C
Survey Consent Example

Following is an example of survey consent. It is only an example and should not be used without checking with your organization's research policies, review board, and government to be sure you comply with applicable laws and policies. Remember that the age of consent may not be the same in all states, provinces, or countries.

*****

University of [Name, Location]

RESEARCH INFORMATION SHEET

You are being asked to participate in the research project described below. Your participation in this study is entirely voluntary and you may refuse to participate, or you may decide to stop your participation at any time. Should you refuse to participate in the study or should you withdraw your consent and stop participation in the study, your decision will involve no penalty or loss of benefits to which you may be otherwise entitled. You are being asked to read the information below carefully, and ask questions about anything you don't understand before deciding whether or not to participate.

Title: [Enter short title here]
Principle Investigator: [Name here]
Student Researcher: [Add here if applicable]

PURPOSE OF THE STUDY
The purpose of the study is to explore … or,
The purpose of this research is to collect information about…

PROCEDURES
We ask you to indicate how much you approve or disapprove of certain behaviors. We then lead you to a questionnaire about your attitudes. We will also ask you about your age, sex, education, and year of birth. Participation in the study will take a total of about 15 minutes.

POTENTIAL RISKS AND DISCOMFORTS
No potential risks are anticipated. If you however feel discomfort in answering certain questions, you are free to skip these questions without consequences of any kind.

POTENTIAL BENEFITS
Although you will not benefit from your participation in this survey, those interested in this research will be able to refer back to the research team's web site at (list site] to see the results.

PAYMENT FOR PARTICIPATION
You will not be paid for your participation in this research study.

CONFIDENTIALITY
This study is entirely anonymous - no identifying information will be collected about you.

PARTICIPATION AND WITHDRAWAL

This study is entirely voluntary. If you volunteer to be in this study, you may end your participation at any time without consequences of any kind. You may also refuse to answer any questions you do not want to answer and still remain in the study. The investigator may withdraw you from this research if circumstances arise which warrant doing so.

IDENTIFICATION OF INVESTIGATORS
If you have any questions or concerns about the research, please feel free to contact the Principal
Investigator:
Name, Position
Department, Organization or University
City, State or Province, Country, Code
Email
Phone

RIGHTS OF RESEARCH SUBJECTS
You may withdraw your consent at any time and discontinue participation without penalty. You are not waiving any legal claims, rights or remedies because of your participation in this research study. If you wish to ask questions about your rights as a research participant or if you wish to voice any problems or concerns you may have about the study to someone other than the researchers, please call [office name and phone number] or write to [name and address].

This project has been certified exempt from IRB review by [name] at [organization or university] IRB#
Please start with the survey now by clicking on the Continue button below.

Appendix D
Survey Debriefing Example

At the conclusion of a survey, researchers should provide respondents with some information about the survey. And it is good policy to thank them for their participation. Check with your organization to see if they have specific guidelines for debriefing survey respondents.

The debriefing should be easy to understand by people who have no background in research methods. Following are some things to include in your statement.

- Describe your hypothesis.
- Sate what deception was used, if any, and why it was needed.
- Tell what the participants in the other conditions did (if applicable).
- State what results the researcher(s) expect(s) to find. Provide contact information so participants can communicate if they have questions.

Following is an example of a debriefing form. Before modifying this form, check with your organization about debriefing requirements.

*****

Debriefing Form
Project Title: [Enter here]
People's perceptions of [topic] vary greatly. Studies have shown, for example, that people are ... [an example].

In this study, we wanted to see if [describe].

We predict that participants will rate [enter your prediction here].

If you have any questions or comments, please contact (name) at (email and/ or telephone number).

If you would like to read more about this topic, [suggest a book or article].

Thank you for your participation!

Appendix E
Organizing a Spreadsheet

Many survey programs include an option to download data into a spreadsheet format. The general approach is to assign people to rows and their responses to columns. To save on long titles for columns, abbreviations are commonly used with longer labels added on printed results. An ID (identification) number is used to protect confidentiality. Age may identify a person in a small group so you may wish to use only one or two age groups. In order to group results in different ways, researchers often need to assign numbers to groups (e.g., women = 1 and men = 2, 0 = Other or prefer not to answer). You can add many social context questions as may be appropriate to your study. Workshop questions are identified as Q1 to Q5. Beneath each question is the rating on a 1 to 5 basis. Long surveys can easily run over 100 columns with 500 rows.

Following is an example of a partial spreadsheet used to evaluate a workshop.

ID	Age	Sex	Q1	Q2	Q3	Q4	Q5
001	19	1	2	3	2	3	4
002	25	1	4	5	4	3	2
003	64	2	3	4	4	5	3
004	33	0	5	4	5	4	2

Many spreadsheet programs calculate statistics, which can appear at the bottom of the columns or elsewhere.

Appendix F
Examples of Survey Items

There is no fee for noncommercial use of the items in this appendix in teaching and research. Many of these items reflect my work in psychology of religion research. Although the items may not apply to many projects, I hope the examples are useful for thinking about how to write items. I also hope more researchers will add the dimension of spirituality to their survey projects. Finally, although most of the spiritual items were written for use with Christians because it is the dominant religion in the United States, many items can be modified to use with adherents of other religions. You do not need additional permission to use these items in teaching or research—just cite the reference provided. For *commercial* use, contact suttongphd@gmail.com.

Christian Beliefs Index (CBI): 4 items
The Christian Beliefs items are rated on a scale from 1 (strongly disagree) to 5 (strongly agree).

1. I have had a born-again experience.
2. God heals some people without human intervention.
3. All Christians are called to share their faith with others.
4. People who do not accept Jesus as their personal savior will spend eternity in hell.

Score the index by adding the values. Scores can range from 4 to 20 unless you use a different metric. In our study, the mean was 18.10 and the standard deviation was 2.19. The skew was

-1.30, which was acceptable (+/- 1.50). Kurtosis was also acceptable (1.61).

Coefficient alpha for our study (Sutton, Arnzen, & Kelly, 2016) was adequate (.74).

Validity data indicate significant positive correlations with other aspects of spirituality, which supports its use as measuring another dimension of the construct, Christian *spirituality*. Following is a table showing the Pearson Correlation Coefficients for the relationship between the Beliefs Index and four other measures of Christian spirituality.

Index or Measure	Correlation
Personal Christian Practices	.25*
Intratextual Fundamentalism Items	.56*
Christian Social Values	.52*
Christian Service Scale	.22*

* $p < .01$

Christian Service Index (CSI): 3 items
The following items are rated on a scale from 1 (strongly disagree) to 5 (strongly agree).

1. I am an effective witness for my faith.
2. I am an effective teacher in a church or small group.
3. I am an effective leader or administrator in a church or small group.

Alpha = .99 and .82 (Sutton, Jordan, Worthington 2014)
Alpha = 78 (Sutton, Arnzen, Kelly, 2016)

Christian Spiritual Gifting: 4 items

The following items are rated on a scale from 1 (strongly disagree) to 5 (strongly agree).

1. I speak in tongues.
2. I interpret tongues spoken by others.
3. I have known things about others that only God could have known.
4. I have spoken a prophesy.

Alpha = .79 (Sutton, Jordan, Worthington 2014)

Marriage

Kansas Marital Satisfaction Scale (KMS): 3-items

Items are rated on a 7-point scale ranging from 1 (extremely dissatisfied) to 7 (extremely satisfied).

1. How satisfied are you with your marriage?
2. How satisfied are you with your husband/wife as a spouse?
3. How satisfied are you with your relationship with your husband/wife?

Alpha = .93 (Schumm et al., 1986)
Walter R. Schumm granted permission to include this scale.

Scoring:

First, reverse the scores for items 2, 5, 6, 8, 9 as follows: "Strongly Disagree" 1 point, "Disagree" 2 points, "Agree" 3 points, and "Strongly Agree" 4 points. Add the scores for all ten items. Higher scores indicate higher self-esteem.

Spiritual Healing Index: 5 items

1. I have been healed of a physical condition.
2. I have been healed of depression or anxiety.
3. I have been delivered from a sinful habit.
4. I have been led by God to pray for the sick or hurting.
5. I have prayed for the sick and they've been healed.

Alpha = .79 (Sutton, Jordan, Worthington 2014)
Alpha = .70 (Sutton, Arnzen, Kelly, 2016)

Spiritual Practices Index

The Spiritual Practices items are rated as follows: 1 never, 2 rarely, 3 sometimes, 4 most of the time, 5 always.

Please tell us a little about your spiritual practices.

1. I study the Bible every week.
2. I pray each day.
3. I attend church almost every week.
4. I regularly support Christian ministry

Score the index by adding the values. Scores can range from 4 to 20 unless you use a different metric. In our study, the mean was 17.51 and the standard deviation was 2.40. The skew was -1.10, which was acceptable (+/- 1.50). Kurtosis was also acceptable (.81).

Coefficient alpha for our study (Sutton et al., 2016) was adequate (.74).

Validity data indicate significant positive correlations with other aspects of spirituality, which supports its use as measuring another dimension of the construct, *spirituality*. Following is a table showing the Pearson Correlation Coefficients for the relationship between the Spirituality Index and four other measures of spirituality.

Index or Measure	Correlation
Christian Beliefs	.25*
Intratextual Fundamentalism Items	.36*
Christian Social Values	.34*
Christian Service Scale	.51*

$* p < .01$

The SPI can be modified for use with people of other religions but we will not know how the items function until a study is conducted with the modified items. A modification follows:

Please tell us a little about your spiritual practices.

I study sacred texts every week.
I pray each day.
I attend a place of worship almost every week.
I regularly support ministries related to my faith.

References for the measures in this appendix

Schumm, W. R., Paff-Bergen, L. A., Hatch, R. C., Obiorah, F. C., Copeland, J. M., Meens, L. D., & Bugaighis, M. A. (1986). Concurrent and discriminant validity of the

Kansas Marital Satisfaction scale. *Journal of Marriage and the Family*, *48*, 381-387.

Sutton, G. W., Arnzen, C., & Kelly, H. (2016). Christian counseling and psychotherapy: Components of clinician spirituality that predict type of Christian intervention. *Journal of Psychology and Christianity*, *35*, 204-214.
Sutton, G. W., Jordan, K., & Worthington, E.L., Jr. (2014). Spirituality, hope, compassion, and forgiveness: Contributions of Pentecostal spirituality to godly love. *Journal of Psychology and Christianity*, *33*, 212-226

Note:

Here's the web address to the International Personality Item Pool: ipip.ori.org

Appendix G

Sample Workshop Evaluation

These items are best suited to online evaluations. They can easily be modified for paper forms by creating checkboxes below the items or in a column to the right of each item.

Consider adding or deleting items to suit your needs. For example, you may want to evaluate how well each objective was accomplished. Similarly, you may want to test for knowledge of specific concepts your instructors taught.

The closed-ended items are designed to be rated on a 5-point scale: 5 = Strongly agree, 4 = Agree, 3 = Neutral, 2 = Disagree, 1 = Strongly disagree.

The open-ended questions require adequate space for participants to enter their comments.

The "select" item requires a "drop down" list but you could ask people to enter the information or provide the title on a printed form.

Consider adding items to evaluate food service if that was included.

*****

Please provide basic information about the workshop.

Enter the date of the workshop.

Select the title of the workshop you attended.

Enter the name of your instructor.

*****

Please rate your overall impressions of the workshop.

1. The quality of this workshop was excellent.

2. Overall, I was highly satisfied with the instructor's presentation.

3. Overall, the facilities were satisfactory.

*****

Please respond to the following items by indicating your agreement or disagreement with the statement.

1. The objectives of the workshop were clearly presented.

2. The topics were relevant to my work.

3. The content was organized and easy to follow.

4. The materials were helpful.

5. The instructor was knowledgeable.

6. The instructor was well prepared.

7. The instructor responded well to questions.

8. Objective # 1 (enter) was met.

9. Objective #2 (enter) was met.

10. Objective #3 (enter) was met.

11. The time allotted to the workshop was sufficient.

12. The meeting room was comfortable.

13. The restrooms were clean and well maintained.

14. The parking was adequate.

*****

Please enter your response to the following questions:

1. What did you like most about the workshop?

2. How could this workshop be improved?

3. What workshops topics would you like see presented in the future?

4. What other comments do you have for the workshop team?

Table of Contents: Expanded

How can you decide between closed and open items?
    Culture
    Writing
    History
What are some guidelines for writing items?
    Meaningfulness
    Readability
    Abstract
    Bias
    Personal
    Ambiguity
How can we use numbers for categories and ratings?
What are some response options?
What are some guidelines for writing open-ended items?
What are some guidelines for writing open-ended items?
How can you obtain items written by others?
An example
Summary
Concepts

4. Organizing and Formatting Surveys   55
  Survey length and time
  Item order
  Survey appearance
  Use of incentives
  Prepare for interviews
        Decide on method
        Recruit and train
        Support interviewers
        Prepare scripts
        Organize practice sessions
        Monitor interviews

C Cognition
    Opinions
    Beliefs
    Attitudes
    Knowledge
O Observable Behavior Patterns—Personality
P Physiology
E Emotions
S Spiritual—Beliefs, Practices, Experiences
Drawing Conclusions About People
Resource Note
Summary
Concepts

Basic Information
    Age
    Sex and Gender
    Education
    Ethnicity and race
    Occupation and Employment
    Income
Relationships
    Family Relationships
    Romantic Relationships
Religious Affiliation
Summary
Concepts

Opinions
Beliefs

Acknowledgments

Thanks to Lois Olena who responded quickly and enthusiastically to an early draft.
Thanks to Johan Mostert whose comments are always encouraging.
Thanks to Shonna Crawford for her generous praise and helpful feedback leading to reorganizing some chapters.
Thanks to Joe Wilmoth for his feedback and recommendation.
Thanks to Luke Davidiuk for his strong endorsement.
Thanks to Beth Barker for editing the manuscript in a timely fashion.

About the Author

Geoffrey W. Sutton is a psychologist, author, and conference speaker. He obtained his Ph.D. in Psychology from the University of Missouri in 1981. He is Emeritus Professor of Psychology of Evangel University in Springfield, Missouri, where he taught courses in research methods, statistics, and the Psychology of Religion. He has published more than 100 books, chapters, and articles. His interests focus on moral psychology and positive psychology variables such as forgiveness, hope, and compassion.

Connections

Book website for Creating Surveys
   https://sites.google.com/view/suttonsurvey/home

Author Website: www.suttong.com

   https://sites.google.com/site/geoffwsuttonphd/home

Twitter: @GeoffWSutton https://twitter.com/GeoffWSutton

Facebook Page: https://www.facebook.com/Geoff.W.Sutton/

Author Page: Geoffrey W. Sutton

Other Books by Geoffrey W. Sutton

A House Divided
Sexuality, Morality, and Christian Cultures

Discussion Guide for A House Divided

Forgiveness, Reconciliation, and Restoration
—Co-edited with Martin Mittelstadt

Christian Morality: An Interdisciplinary Framework for
Thinking About Contemporary Moral Issues
—Co-edited with Brandon Schmidly

Applied Statistics
Concepts for Counselors

Made in the USA
Middletown, DE
06 January 2020